THREESCORE
AND MORE

THREESCORE
AND MORE

Applying the Assets of Maturity, Wisdom, and Experience for Personal and Professional Success

ALAN WEISS

"We don't stop playing games because we grow old; we grow old because we stop playing games."

—George Bernard Shaw

"Musicians don't retire; they simply run out of music."

—Louis Armstrong

First edition published in 2017
by Bibliomotion, Inc.
711 Third Avenue New York, NY 10017, USA
2 Park Square, Milton Park, Abingdon, Oxon OX14 4RN, UK

Bibliomotion is an imprint of Taylor & Francis Group, an Informa business

No claim to original U.S. Government works

Printed on acid-free paper

International Standard Book Number-13: 978-1-138-55816-8 (Hardback)
International Standard Book Number-13: 978-1-315-15128-1 (eBook)

Library of Congress Cataloging-in-Publication Data

Title: Threescore and more : applying the assets of maturity, wisdom, and
experience for personal and professional success / Alan Weiss.
Description: New York, NY : Routledge, 2018. | Includes index.
Identifiers: LCCN 2017051267 | ISBN 9781138558168 (hardback : alk. paper)
Subjects: LCSH: Weiss, Alan, 1946- author. | Older people--United
States--Attitudes. | Older people--United States--Social conditions. |
Stereotypes (Social psychology)--United States. | Maturation
(Psychology)--United States. | Self-actualization (Psychology)--United
States.
Classification: LCC HQ1064.U6 W37 2018 | DDC 305.260973--dc23
LC record available at https://lccn.loc.gov/2017051267

Visit the Taylor & Francis Web site at
http://www.taylorandfrancis.com
Printed and bound in the United States of America by Sheridan

Contents

Chapter Overview

Introduction

Chapter 1: The Myth of Boomers, Greatest Generations, Millennials, and Gen-Anything

- It's ironic that we praise diversity, but create homogenization.
- My father's mantra when he was shot at: It won't be me.
- Maturity is the great gift of age.
- You may not be what you eat, but you are who you hang out with.

Current cultural and normative pressures tend to degrade the image and abilities of those above a certain age, and these people therefore suddenly begin to believe what they're told instead of abiding by their own experiences. There is a demeaning, offensive undercurrent in a "senior discount" and even in the word "senior."

Chapter 2: The Future Began Yesterday

- Each day is a new page in your story.
- A legacy is a journey, not an ending.
- You *can* make up lost ground.
- The future is not a different version of today.

We tend to equate "legacy" with what we leave to our children and grandchildren. But our legacy is actually daily, and our duty is to keep adding to and improving it. Many people in the arts and business didn't flourish until well into their seventies and beyond. When people aren't forced to retire (by law or by rule or by their own mindset), they can make great strides.

Chapter 3: Power Increases with Age

- Maximizing and utilizing travel and experiences
- Improving and expanding language
- Knowledge is for kids: Creating wisdom
- The value of healthy selfishness and comfort

The image of grandparents sacrificing their own lives to take care of their grandchildren while their children hold down two jobs (or simply take vacations) has to be smashed. Age does not suggest involuntary servitude (based on guilt), nor the obligation to make your children wealthy from your own assets. Power actually increases with age, and we might as well feel free and get good at applying it.

Chapter 4: Biceps, Quads, and Self-Esteem Are All Muscles

- Daily workouts on self-worth
- The "state of confidence" has all the electoral votes.
- Becoming consistent amid inconsistency
- Achieving self-validation

As we age, we tend to look in all the wrong places for validation—our friends, our children, our spouses. That is a surrender of basic power and potential. Older people work out in gyms, ride bikes, run, play tennis, and so forth. So, too, should they work on their self-esteem and mental well-being. We are not what the media, advertisers, young people, or the government tells us. We are who we are (I am who I am), which has worked for both Popeye and God.

Chapter 5: Critical Thinking Is Redundant

- Occam's Razor and the beauty of directness
- Finding causes, not blame
- Exploiting change
- Methodical innovation

Every old dog I've ever had learned new tricks if the tricks were in its self-interest. ALL thinking should be critical thinking, and we should streamline it so we can escape old norms (blaming people long since removed from our lives). There are excellent techniques to remain forceful and innovative in one's thinking and implementation. As we grow older, we need to move from dealing with change to creating it.

Chapter 6: The Nongovernment Safety Net

- The colleagues to acquire and sustain
- Personal support systems for the ages
- The community of your own creation
- Why money is not wealth (and what is)

We shut ourselves up in gated communities and condos where we only look at each other. After having children, we act as if we never want them living near us again. We become nondiverse and herd-like. But there are simple techniques to ensure that new energy keeps entering one's "system" and that we can be self-supporting and interact with a diverse community of our own making—virtually and in reality.

Chapter 7: Forgiveness Is *Not* Easier Than Simply Appropriating Permission

- The range of permissions we allow and deny ourselves
- Removing fear
- Extirpating guilt
- The new *carpe diem*

We deny ourselves based on some real or even imagined societal dictate on what we can do and how we can act, from sexual intimacy to driving, from travel to health care. The way out of this maze is to chop through it and take command of our own lives. We need to stop being victims seeking special treatment (seats reserved for the elderly) and start being independent entrepreneurs creating our own personalized treatment.

Chapter 8: Eliminating Scarcity in Your Soul

- Physical health
- Emotional health
- Psychological health
- Intellectual health

The key to powerful aging is powerful growth. The laws of entropy erode plateaus, so we must keep advancing and climbing, which is an alien concept to many because our society doesn't think it appropriate past a certain age. These are the four critical areas to healthy growth that need ongoing attention and development.

Chapter 9: Healthy Outrage

- How to vent
- Ego restraint
- Tolerance
- Forgiveness

We are often enslaved to people because we hold a grudge over a perceived slight. Yet that person is unaware, so they can't "free" us, and we remain trapped. There are healthy techniques to choose your fights, vent pressure, and salve your ego. Most of all, there is tolerance and forgiveness, which come with maturity and lead you to understand that the idiot who didn't use the signal when turning in front of you was not out to get you.

Chapter 10: Defying Age

- Dealing with inevitable loss
- The difference between pain and suffering
- Spirituality
- Intimacy

Pain is unavoidable in aging, but suffering is voluntary. Our losses may be familial, collegial, or even related to abilities, but they can be overcome and used as strengths. Our relationships to the world around us and to others are the crucial elements in sustaining and improving our strengths while accommodating our losses. Why are we opposed to suicide yet so often sacrifice life piecemeal on a daily basis?

Introduction

At birth, the average life expectancy among the well-supported English peerage in late medieval times was 30. In more modern England, during the 17th century or so, it was 33–40. In 1900, the world average was 31, and in 1950, it was 48 (that is *not* a typo).[1] Yet in ancient Greece, people routinely lived into their 70s, about the same as in current Western countries. (Socrates died at 70 by execution, not old age.)

We have healthy optimism about a long life, yet we also know that it can be cut tragically short by accident, disease, natural disaster, or crime. Despite that, and despite what is a fairly general condemnation of suicide and euthanasia, we think little of throwing life away piecemeal by procrastinating, not taking advantage of opportunities, and vacillation.

The question becomes: Is a nonproductive life of 80 years better than a highly productive one of 50?

What we do know is that we have a precariously brief time on this planet. The dinosaurs flourished for about 125 million years—more than you and I can imagine—compared with perhaps 10,000 for modern humans. And the dinosaurs would still be the dominant life-form if an annihilating asteroid hadn't crashed into the Gulf of Mexico.

So where does that leave us?

One frightening factor I've observed in more than 30 years of global travel while consulting with organizations in over 50 countries is that, especially in America, we do not honor people as they age. In fact, we tend to cast them aside, assuming that their skills diminish, their contributions cease, and their wisdom wanes. Inuits who put their elders on ice floes to die so as to feed polar bears were few and far apart, and the last recorded case was in 1939.[2]

Yet a form of senicide exists today, and it entails far more than the obvious—the nursing homes that lack proper care, social service safety nets with holes in them, the extinction of the extended family. And it exists at a much younger age than we think.

If you are over 50, or concerned about approaching 50, and the American Association of Retired People (AARP) keeps berating you to join, this book is about you. There is an invidious disease in American life that robs people of their power and respect as they age for no reason other than bias. In fact, at this writing, ageism is one of the three basic biases in our society that no one spends much time protesting.[3] And by the way, about half of retirees in a recent survey reported that retirement was either only "moderately satisfying" or "not satisfying at all." Working longer improves satisfaction and also helps you live longer.[4] Hence, what follows in these pages demonstrates how to aggressively retain *and build* your power as you age. Not as you "grow old," but simply as time passes. As you'll see as you read on, we are undermined and weakened daily by forced retirements, characterizations, assumptions of weakness, blanket "seniors" offerings, and walled communities.

We talk about "hitting 50" or "approaching 60" as though we're sailing between Scylla and Charybdis. I don't know about you, but as I look back I'm appalled by what I thought and how I behaved in my twenties. I was immature in my thirties. But I hit my stride in my forties and am at the top of my game in my early seventies. TOP OF MY GAME!

While those of us who feel that way may be said to have good genes or strong resources or simply a lucky life, I think it's primarily a fact of refusing to surrender power and resisting the normative pressure to become a statistic or stereotype.

If you're interested in growing stronger in your life and career as you awake each morning, then follow me. I'm not interested in anyone who'd rather stay in bed.

Alan Weiss, PhD
East Greenwich, Rhode Island
November 2017

Historical Fact

In August 1935, the Social Security Act was passed by Congress to establish old-age benefits for workers, aid for victims of work-related accidents, unemployment insurance, and aid for widowed mothers, children, the blind, and the physically disabled. It was one of relatively few pieces of Franklin D. Roosevelt's New Deal legislation to be both passed by Congress and upheld by the courts.

Over the years, the system grew to include farm and domestic workers, the self-employed, and others. Cost-of-living adjustments were added in 1972. By 1983, social security funds faced exhaustion.

At the program's outset, approximately 14 people were working and contributing money to the system for every retired person who would qualify for benefits. The retirement age was 65, as it is for much of the workforce today, 85 years later, but the average lifespan at that time was 68. Today, a 65-year-old can expect to live to about 84, on average.

And today, only 2.5 workers contribute to the system for every retired person. We've gone from 14 people contributing to a 3-year retirement duration to fewer than 3 people contributing to *a 20-year retirement duration*. Of course the system is exhausted, because the math no longer works. It's as if we said that if an airplane can carry 300 passengers for 4 hours, there's no reason to believe it can't carry 1200 people for 8 hours.

Moreover, the original concept of social security was to provide additional benefits to augment one's personal savings, retirement funds, extended family support, community services, part-time work, and so on—not to support a lifestyle. The majority of today's baby boomers, however, average less than $100,000 in personal retirement funds, don't qualify for community services, no longer have extended families capable or willing to help, and have focused on spending, not saving.

The answer to this quandary is not to try to enhance social security funding nor to change the basic rules of math and replace them with some Utopian algorithm that makes all this disappear.

The answer is to understand that "retirement" is a silly artifact and that people not only can but should be expected to contribute to society for their own fulfillment and income on an ongoing basis.

"Retirement" literally means "withdrawal to a place of seclusion."

If you're not familiar with the famous Dylan Thomas poem about fighting the dying light, visit Poets.org to read it (https://www.poets.org/poetsorg/poem/do-not-go-gentle-good-night).

Notes

1. "Life Expectancy," Wikipedia, https://en.wikipedia.org/wiki/Life_expectancy.
2. "Did Eskimos Put Their Elderly on Ice Floes to Die?" Straight Dope, May 4, 2004, http://www.straightdope.com/columns/read/2160/did-eskimos-put-their-elderly-on-ice-floes-to-die.
3. The others being biases against obesity and religious beliefs in a secular society, but those are for other books.
4. Study by the Employee Benefit Research Institute, reported in the *Chicago Tribune*, July 8, 2017.

CHAPTER 1

The Myth of Boomers, Greatest Generation, Millennials, and Gen-Anything

Current cultural and normative pressures tend to degrade the image and abilities of those above a certain age, and these people therefore suddenly begin to believe what they're told instead of abiding by their own experiences. There is a demeaning, offensive undercurrent in a "senior discount" and even in the word "senior."

It's Ironic That We Praise Diversity but Create Homogenization

We profess to love inclusion these days, but that's basically a politically correct philosophy meant to embrace ethnicity, skin color, origins, disabilities, and sexual identities. What's actually transpired is that we've become a tribalized society. Recently, I've heard of separate graduation exercises for black and LGBT students.

Instead of a melting pot and a society in which people seek the mainstream, we've become a tribal, fragmented society, with hyphens to carry separate identities on our journeys and special recognitions of the first of our "tribe" to reach certain goals (first openly gay mayor, first African-American Academy Award winner, first woman in space, first Latino in the Senate, and so forth).

Yet aging, which the ancients regarded as the accomplishment of wisdom and mature reasoning, well, it's not celebrated so much. When Tom

Wolfe wrote *The Kingdom of Speech* (he's 86 and the author of, among other books, *The Right Stuff* and *Bonfire of the Vanities*), *New York Times* reviewer Caitlin Flanagan included a line about "an old man's willingness to digress." I'm sure if Ms. Flanagan had read a line by someone else that referred to "a woman's willingness to digress" we would never hear the end of it. But Wolfe's (brilliant) book and writing could be demeaned because, in the reviewer's limited perspective, he was somewhere north of his dotage.[1] (I believe Ms. Flanagan is herself in her fifties, which is an indication that we tend to both deny that we're "old" yet condemn those who are older.)

I recall a *New Yorker* cartoon in which an interviewer said to the job candidate, "I don't know what it is about you, but I instantly like you!" The two men looked exactly alike.

One of our tribal attributes today is that like attracts like. People at a certain standard of living tend to live with and near others of that same standard of living, not by default (ghettos) but by choice (walled communities). We have, with virtually no protest, groups such as the Women's Executive Council, the Ebony Awards, gay pride parades, and the Paralympics. We also treat the "aged" specially: with forced retirements, rejection for decent jobs, and tougher insurance criteria.

American companies routinely lay off their senior people—who, through years of loyal contribution have reached appropriate, predetermined pay grades—and replace them with young people who can be paid a fraction of their salaries. We create senior tours for golf and tennis on the assumption that, past a certain age, you can't win on the regular circuits. Yet Julius Boros won the PGA championship at 48 (beating Arnold Palmer), and Kazuyoshi Miura is a star Japanese soccer player at 50. Bernard Hopkins, 51, retired after 28 years in professional boxing, having won the WBC title at 46 and successfully defended it twice at 48 and 49.

I mention these figures because they are in the world of sports, where conditioning, strength, and stamina are so important. But let's face it, the world of business, education, and government require no such physical prowess—only intelligence, judgment, and critical thinking skills.

We tend to deny those of certain ages inclusion, let alone respect, even though the world has changed along with the actuarial calculations used for social security and safety nets. For example, I remember my father-in-law actually burning the mortgage papers on his $8000 house when he paid off the 30-year loan in the 1960s.

Today, people over 70 routinely refinance and procure new mortgages. *Even when they can afford to pay cash, they take out a mortgage!* About 42 percent of households headed by someone between 65 and 74 have home-secured debt.[2] This number was 18.5 percent in 1992 and 32 percent in 2004.

An estimated 10,000 people a day are turning (as we say) 65.

And while banks are very careful about loans to "older" customers—with more paperwork, a higher deposit required, and evidence of more assets demanded—this field is growing dramatically. The IRS legislation of the Reagan years (our oldest president at the time) is now releasing trillions of dollars into the economy, the largest transfer of wealth in the history of the country (and perhaps the world), as baby boomers create legacies for their families.

It's important to note that not all bias against people above certain ages is externally created, although the bias is encouraged by our society. We have communities that are "child free," cruises and other recreation that demand a certain minimum age, and varied activities that are restricted in one way or another.

Yet …

I know too many people who have retired and accepted their pensions, social security, and retirement plans and giddily stayed home … and waited to die. In some professions retirement comes insanely young—firefighters, police officers, members of the military. Yet I can understand putting in 20 years, emerging at 40, and beginning a second career because you've served the community and the country, often in dangerous pursuits, and have earned it.

What I have difficulty understanding is why people retire in their late fifties or early sixties—an "early out"—and thereafter do virtually nothing. How many gardens can you tend? How much peace do you need? How long can you play with grandchildren? And how many of those accursed, buffet-heavy cruises can you withstand?

Barring disease, accident, and natural disaster, at 65 we're going to live for another 20 or more years—84.3, to be exact, as of this writing.[3] (And at 84, you'll live another 7 years, on average, with the main cause of death being cancer.)[4] Isn't it wiser to take a holistic view of life and not plan by the decade or generation (more about that later) and simply see ourselves as vital, contributing humans not bound by some archaic norm about what we should or can be doing at various periods of our growth?

John Adams was 90, Thomas Jefferson 83, and Benjamin Franklin 84 when they died, contributing (and arguing and provoking) right up to the end of their lives, in far harsher times than we endure today. They founded a country and a historic experiment in democracy and freedom. The least we can do is continue to create and contribute for as long as possible.

Nearly a quarter of all physicians in America are now 65 or older, and 40 percent of them see patients daily. Older doctors have lower rates of malpractice claims and lower "never events," meaning instances in which they operated on the wrong person or the wrong body part.[5]

My Father's Mantra When He Was Shot At: It Won't Be Me

My father is of the cohort Tom Brokaw wrote about in *The Greatest Generation*,[6] a paean to those who grew up in the Great Depression and went on to fight and win World War II. Brokaw's contention is that no group was ever called upon for such sacrifice and heroism.

My father enlisted in the Army before Pearl Harbor and volunteered for the first parachute regiment ever formed. It was so dangerous that only volunteers were accepted. They jumped at first with no reserve chute from cargo planes flying quite low. (I guess they thought the impact of dropping from 500 feet was less lethal than from 1,000 feet.)

Once the war began, his unit was shipped to Australia and they were dropped over Lae, New Guinea, to try to halt the Japanese advance toward Australia. A great many of the men in his unit were killed, but they succeeded in their mission.

I asked him when I was younger how he could do that.

"You just never think it's going to be you," he explained, as if telling me that the car needed gas. My father died at 99 years and 11 months of age, spending his last 2 days in a hospital kidding with the nurses, then dying in his sleep.

A lot of people think, "It will be me." They think this on their jobs when there are cutbacks. They think this when they're told, "Two out of three of you won't graduate." They think this when they have a mole and visit the doctor, certain that it's cancer. (A 68-year-old colleague told me that every 90 days he visits his doctor's office, where they remove still another cancerous lesion from his face. "It's a fine system," he says, and goes about leading a highly successful firm.)

The degree to which you believe positive outcomes will result or negative outcomes are inevitable informs your behavior. You're bolder and more confident if you expect the best. You're timid and less carefree if you expect the worst. You can see this on the athletic field, both in team sports and individual performances. Tom Brady won the Super Bowl with the Patriots in 2017—his fifth, at 39, "old" in football—having been behind by a record number of points (25) after the first half.

He knew what he and the team could do. The defeated Falcons became more inept as the game wore on, losing confidence in a vicious cycle until they were defeated in overtime. In sports, some stars call for the ball in pressure situations, and some avoid it at all costs.

Let's first dispel the notion of generational attributes. We talk in terms of "boomers" (I'm of the eldest group of boomers), "Gen X," "millennials," and so forth. In so doing, we assign common attributes to vast numbers of disparate people, thereby treating them with a broad brush.

A generation in America at present would involve about 70 million people. That's about the population of Germany, or of Canada and Australia combined. Generations may have unique collective opportunities—in terms of new technologies, for example—but the individuals within a generation also have their nurturing, their education, and the chemistry of heredity coursing through their veins, which all add to their unique perspectives and personalities.

Yet instead of relying our own experiences, we tend to believe what we're told about our experiences! This phenomenon reminds me of the admonition "Who are you going to believe, me or your lying eyes?"

As we age, we tend to believe what we're told about our generation and ourselves. We become less like individuals and more like herd animals unless we resist. At work we're told that we're declining in our productivity and energy and creativity. Innovation is a young person's game. Our memes and reference points become unquestioned truths rather than individual occurrences.

Here is a case in point: Willy Loman is the aging protagonist in the classic play *Death of a Salesman*.[7] He's the "smile and a shoeshine" sales guy who charms his customers, until his customers change and his younger colleagues employ more aggressive skills. He dies on the job, refusing to adjust his style (because, presumably, he's unable), and his wife eventually screams in a famous scene, "Attention must be paid!"

Willy Loman is the epitome of the aging, unchanging person who is doomed by the passage of time and inability to adjust. He's the stegosaurus whose asteroid is actually modernity.

Yet, my experience in corporate America is vastly different from the portrait presented in the play. The older people in most positions possess experience that no one else does, because you don't learn experience in school any more than you learn to ride a bicycle by reading a book.

You may be wondering how real the phenomenon is: In organizational life, is the power of maturity truly underestimated and underappreciated? Here's an example.

I was consulting on performance and productivity with Atlantic Electric in Cape May County, New Jersey. One day, one of the executives casually mentioned to me that they were downsizing because of technology advances but were doing so "humanely" by offering lucrative early retirement packages.

"Why don't you let me investigate that a bit, just to be sure?" I offered. He was reluctant, having had human resources guarantee that this was the path other companies had taken. But I was eager for more work and also dubious of the nonspecific "humane" offer, and I finally prevailed.

In the next 48 hours, I discovered that every veteran linesman—everyone over 50 with at least 20 years on the job—was going to accept the package, meaning there would be *no one left to rig high wires in an ice storm*. It can get very mean in southern New Jersey in the winter, and Atlantic Electric was responsible for providing power to every casino in Atlantic City. The loss of that capability would have been devastating.

The initiative was quickly cancelled, and my star shone. But most importantly, it became evident that a quantitative view of people (as in generational titles and attributes) was woefully insufficient. A *qualitative* view of people was required.

On the job, and in life, we need to make our talents known, our contributions recognized, our results manifest. That's because the tropism is toward clumping everyone together in generational drawers and broad-brush painting older people with age-related limitations. We think it harmless to talk about the early bird patrons at retirement destinations driving cars too big for them too slowly in the high-speed lanes.

No doubt some do that. Just as some Gen Xers took 6 years to earn a degree that took others only 4, and some millennials drive under the influence. But those results are exceptions, not embedded in generational DNA.

My father was right: You behave assuming the best for yourself, and that, in most cases, will result in the best for yourself.

Maturity Is the Great Gift of Age

The song "The Second Time Around" has a line that says, "Love, like youth, is wasted on the young."[8] Tom Stoppard, the great playwright, observed, "Age is a very high price to pay for maturity."

Maturity can be defined as having reached a point in life of emotional and character development consistent with responsible, adult behavior. It is also used euphemistically to describe someone of middle age or more, as in "She was a mature person when she set the mountain climbing ascent record."

Maturity, *per se*, is a judgmental state. We know young people "mature beyond their years" and we know quite immature older people (particularly the uncle who gets drunk at the Christmas party every year). However, it does make sense that maturity should increase with age and that there is a maturation process that requires time. Teachers often find that even child prodigies, capable of entering college at 12, require a socialization process if they're to be truly healthy. We've worked with a charter school specializing in sending economically disadvantaged inner-city kids to excellent high schools—with a staggering success rate in high school and subsequently college admission (98 percent)—but found that the kids needed socialization to help them thrive in those new environments.

In fact, many people recognized as "savants" appear to be quite immature in all other ways. Vince Lombardi, the legendary football coach ("Winning isn't the important thing, it's the only thing," he was rumored to have proclaimed) was a horrible father and husband. His maturity was limited to football.[9] Steve Jobs was certainly emblematic of this discordance,[10] as is Tiger Woods as I write these words. These men were brilliant within a narrow pursuit but incredibly immature in dealing with the rest of the world.

What has this to do with us, our aging, the world of work, and our lives in general?

Have you ever realized that someone else provided a more mature response than you did (or vice versa) to a common question or problem? Have you found yourself seeking the counsel of some but not others? Do you notice that some people successfully tuck their ego away while others wear it like the figurehead on the bow of an old sailing frigate?

Maturity is a key aspect of success because it provides perspective, temperance, measured responses, and appropriate situational behavior (there are times to turn the other cheek and times to be healthily outraged). Here are the ingredients of maturity as I've observed them in thousands of coaching assignments and interactions.

- **Experiences.** The more experiences we have, the more perspective we have. Seeing the Great Wall of China in photographs, for example, is nowhere close in impact to seeing the structure and walking on it yourself in person. That's because the hugeness of the thing can't be conveyed accurately in photos, nor can a touchdown pass on television or the unfettered joy at a wedding reception. As we gather our personal experiences, we add to our critical thinking ability and our judgment. People who refuse to travel confound me, and those who travel and insist on eating the same food every night no matter where they are might as well have stayed at home.

- **Socialization.** I love dogs, and dogs do best when raised with their litter mates. They develop a "puppy bite," which they retain throughout their lives, from their play routines. My 80-pound German Shepherd, who could take down a deer, plays with my granddaughters gleefully, nipping them but never, ever biting hard (and these dogs have some of the strongest jaw pressures of all animals). Their socialization early on provides these important traits. Dogs raised in isolation never develop a puppy bite, and don't have that kind of discretion. Maturity is dependent on the ability to "play well with (diverse) others."

- **Education.** Formal education is almost irrelevant here; I'm talking about street smarts. As we age, we learn which techniques work (compromise) and which don't (a punch in the face). Sociopaths, of course, don't, but most people do. Most important—and something formal education is increasingly deficient in providing—is the ability to learn how to learn. These days, issues that we once laboriously looked up or memorized are available via Google or, more simply, Alexa. Content isn't as important these days because it's readily available, but *the process of learning* is the key to our success in rapidly changing workplaces and society as a whole.

- **Ego.** A healthy ego is important, but a runaway ego is perhaps the biggest telltale sign of immaturity. A healthy ego manifests by
  - Sharing credit and accepting blame
  - Showing tolerance and forgiveness (instead of harboring grudges and taking umbrage)
  - Understanding that others don't have to lose for you to win
  - Realizing that there is no need to engage in one-upmanship
  - Standing resolutely for principles but not tastes

Self-esteem provides for a healthy ego. Lack of self-esteem creates an imposter syndrome, in which you believe someone will find out you're not really that good. Acting is a notoriously insecure profession (you're rewarded for portraying someone else) that both of my kids are involved with on both sides of the camera. Those actors holding the Oscars and other awards are often wondering at the same time if they'll ever work again. On the job, we wonder if we merit the promotion, are worthy of the increase, are immune to cutbacks.

Mature people tend to generalize good news. They say, "I'm a great sales-person," instead of, "I was lucky to get that sale." And they confine bad news. They say, "I didn't make that sale to her today on these terms," instead of, "I'm a lousy marketer." Immature people with low self-esteem reverse that.

This is vital in raising kids, by the way. "You missed a tough ball" is better than "You're awkward on the field," and "You're a scholar" is far better than "Well, you did well on *that* test." Ask yourself what your words are to your family, your colleagues, and, most importantly, yourself.[11]

Here's a test for you: In Figure 1.1, evaluate where you are on each trait of maturity. A 3 means you're highly educated (including street smarts), have a rich variety of experiences, are comfortable in diverse social situations, and have a strong, controlled ego. A 2 means the statement is partially true of you. And a 1 means you fare poorly in that area.

Ideally, connecting your ratings with a line will give you a diamond shape at the perimeter of the figure. If your self-evaluation yields less than that,

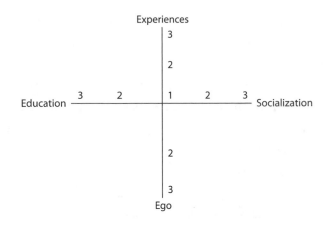

Figure 1.1 *Maturity analysis.*

determine how your education, experiences, socialization, and/or ego need to be further developed and refined, and arrange for the appropriate actions.

Maturity isn't a crapshoot or an accident. It's a conscious, intentional effort that is not the product of age but easier to achieve as we age *if* we pay attention to using it as a strength in life and at work.

You May Not Be What You Eat, but You Are Who You Hang Out With

One of the great influences on our development is our early nurturing—from our parents, our environment, siblings, friends, and so forth. We're fairly helpless about those factors as young children but are much more in control as adults.

Yet we often surrender control.

It's vital to be a part of groups and organizations in which diversity is the norm. That diversity must include age. As we get older, we tend to segregate ourselves with others who have common reference points (hence the generational emphasis that hounds us), common preferences (music), common conditions (empty nests), and even common ailments (high blood pressure).

We need youth in our lives. We need to interact with people younger (and older) than ourselves. Gated retirement communities are a limbo in which people wait for death. Here's a symptom: If over 50 percent of all your conversations are about golf and medical conditions, you're simply in the waiting room for the end of days. Why don't you have more diverse issues to discuss? Because you're hanging out only with people who share those issues, so what else is there to discuss?

And some of you don't play golf!

The institutional memory of organizations is lodged in the most senior people. That holds true for families, companies, nonprofits, civic organizations, educational institutions, and so forth. The reason that families tell the same stories over and over at every holiday party—or employees at every office party—is that we are passing on the learnings of our tribe, repeating them and reinforcing them, so that they continue to provide perspective for others.

At FedEx the (probably apocryphal) story of founder Fred Smith saving an early payroll by winning a poker game is famous, and at Hewlett-Packard the one-car garage in which Bill Hewlett and Dave Packard began their company is legend. Families talk about the time Aunt Margie thought she had won the lottery or the dog ate the Thanksgiving turkey.

Digression

Whether or not you are religious, the Bible, as a literary work, offers a collection of stories and parables meant to convey values and ethical behaviors. Oral histories passed down were compiled by a series of authors into written form. While some people believe that the Bible is literally the word of God, scholars agree that it is in fact a compilation of oral teachings and a remembrance of events.

Oral storytelling, often later transcribed into print, has a long history of providing institutional memory.

What does the need for storytelling and parables mean for us today, in business and life? If we don't want to surrender power or be seen as a cohort of marginalized people, we have to break the herd mentality. Living together and/or working together in homogenous groups is neither productive nor healthy. We don't want to be labeled—through our own actions—as "the elderly" or "seniors." And we don't want to be invisible.

This means that we have to constantly take on new friends who are younger than we are, new colleagues at work, new activities that involve diverse groups. There is a substantial tropism driving people who are over certain ages to be in certain groups. Economic hardship might drive someone to accept or request a senior discount or the early bird special, but if you don't need the small savings, why would you seek it?

We're besieged with the facts that people born after a certain age never used a rotary phone or even a landline and that email is obsolete, having given way to texting. I'm convinced, conversely, that many of the sincere young people who ardently supported Bernie Sanders's presidential bid were completely ignorant of the true basis and weaknesses of socialism, not having been alive when it flourished and crashed.

I'm constantly coaching younger people. (In fact, I find myself in a couple of cases coaching the second generation of my clients!) Tony Bennett is singing with Lady Gaga. The president of France elected in 2017, Emmanuel Macron, is 24 years younger than his wife. It's imperative for all of us *not* to restrict ourselves to others who are like us. If we do, we fall into a trap of commiseration that often sounds like this:

- "It's not like the old days."
- "I'm glad I'm not raising kids today."
- "What can you do but get along as best you can?"
- "Nobody is going to listen to me."

This is the self-reinforcing marginalization of people who only want to be with others like them.

I invited the writer and management consultant Margaret Wheatley to speak at one of my conferences. She and I are the same age, had the same clients many years ago, and had colleagues in common. I think her book *Leadership and the New Science* is fascinating.[12]

Yet her advice to the group was this: Only speak with those who agree with you; it's senseless to try to convert or influence anyone else. She was a 1960s activist, and I believe she thinks all of those efforts failed and we're in a hopeless society. I, however, believe every day brings hope and optimism and endless opportunity.

I asked the group, when we reviewed her work, would you rather follow her or me? Would you rather have her attitude or mine when you face a prospect, a job promotion, or a personal challenge? Do you want to wake up every morning resigned to your fate or eager to create your destiny?

Those questions are not rhetorical. We should ask and answer them daily. If we isolate ourselves and our beliefs by belonging only to certain clubs, participating in certain social activities, and adhering to informal group norms, we create the very stereotypes that society uses to label people, and the default label for people over a certain age is not usually kind.

This chapter has been the stage-setter for the recommendations, behaviors, and actions that follow in the rest of the book. Be critically aware that we control our fate and retain power only if we refuse to be stereotyped and to accept the "herd" labels that society, through the media, insists upon.

Maturity, competency, contribution, success—these are not age related. They are, in fact, reliant on your view of your life.

Notables

Peter Roget, 73. Published the *Thesaurus of English Words and Phrases*.
Ronald Reagan, 70. Became president of the United States.
Frank McCourt, 65. Wrote the Pulitzer Prize–winning memoir *Angela's Ashes*.

Patrick O'Brian, 94. Was working on his 21st book in his *Master and Commander* series when he died.

Jessica Tandy, 80. Won the Academy Award for Best Actress.

Dorothy Davenhill Hirsch, 89. Visited the North Pole.

Lt. Col. James C. Warren, 87. Received his pilot's license.

John Glenn, 77. Traveled in space.

Tony Bennett, 91. Toured with, among others, Lady Gaga.

Notes

1. Alan Weiss, letter to the editor, *New York Times Book Review*, September 4, 2016. The *Times* had the good grace to print my letter to the editor condemning this kind of insidious ageism bias.
2. All mortgage figures are from "Mortgages for Seniors? Available, but Exacting," *New York Times*, June 4, 2017, p. 3, business section.
3. Average lifespan at 65 years old.
4. "84 Year Old Life Expectancy," Health Grove, http://life-span.healthgrove.com/l/85/84.
5. Study by the American Medical Association as reported in "When Are Doctors Too Old?", *Wall Street Journal*, June 26, 2017.
6. Tom Brokaw, *The Greatest Generation*, Random House, New York, 1998.
7. Arthur Miller, *Death of a Salesman*, 1949.
8. Sammy Cahn and Jimmy Van Heusen, 1960, from the film *High Time*.
9. See, for example, David Maraniss, *When Pride Still Mattered*, Simon & Schuster, New York, 1999.
10. Walter Isaacson, *Steve Jobs*, Simon & Schuster, New York, 2011.
11. For more on positive language, see Martin Seligman, *Learned Optimism*, Simon & Schuster, New York, 2011.
12. Margaret Wheatley, *Leadership and the New Science*, Berrett-Koehler, Oakland, CA, 1994.

CHAPTER 2

The Future Began Yesterday

We tend to equate "legacy" with what we leave to our children and grandchildren. But our legacy is actually daily, and our duty is to keep adding to and improving it. Many people in the arts and business didn't flourish until well into their seventies and beyond. When people aren't forced to retire (by law or by rule or by their own mindset), they can make great strides.

Each Day Is a New Page in Your Story

We have a tendency to look to the distant future for our legacy to take shape. But the fact is that we're creating that legacy every day.

Each day, we write a new page in our personal autobiography. The question is, how interesting and appealing is the book? Is each page the same as the one preceding, or are we creating a coherent picture of a maturing, contributing, valuable life?

If you're the owner of a business and you want your business to be sold and provide a valuable annuity for you—in other words, a high valuation for a buyer—you can't wait until the week (or even the year) you intend to sell it to increase that valuation. You have to begin *today* to ensure your firm is valuable and growing in appeal.

If you're in organizational life and you seek advancement, you can't wait until a job opens up to build your résumé and gain experience. You should begin that process now so that you can be opportunistic when appropriate.

As your own life unfolds, you'll notice a tendency to put off things you can do now and experience now to that distant ambiguous future. In your twenties you have all time in the world. In your thirties you realize that it was better to wait, you're wiser now, you can wait a little more, although you have a lot more responsibilities. In your forties you're tied to a career that requires considerable investment to create and maintain. In your fifties you begin to realize you'd better set some priorities. At three score and more, you begin to resign yourself to the fact that some things may not happen.

I know I'm painting a bleak picture, and many people free themselves of this time trap. But too many find themselves wallowing in it like the extinct creatures that sank in the La Brea Tar Pits. The more we struggle, the more we sink in the quicksand of time.

What's happening, of course, is the horizon is getting closer. That distant, hardly perceptible line demarking the border of sea and sky has become more delineated, more visible, more imposing. We still have room between us and the horizon, but we realize it's shrunk and there's less of it.

This drives us from our propensity to think, "There's plenty of time" to "There's still time, but for what?" We've heard the bromide about no one on their deathbed wishing they had spent more time in the office. But what we don't acknowledge is that most people don't fear death so much as they regret the things they never got around to doing.

That's why our book has to have new pages daily, new chapters monthly. We can't stop the approach of the horizon, but we can fill the distance with productivity and contributions instead of swimming aimlessly.

We fall into ruts, into what I call the "success trap." We tend to feather our nest rather than look for and build new ones. We become content and then complacent. We get too comfortable.

That's why stories of unlikely people running marathons, becoming prominent artists, and continuing to run businesses are so popular. They're proof that life doesn't end with a feathered nest. Otherwise, we develop a fear of flying.

We don't live a personal life and a business life. We simply live a life, which is a blend of many pursuits. There is no such thing as "life balance" because there is no perfect formula. But we do tend to go through stages where we're focused on our learning, then a partner, then children, then supporting the family, then the empty nest, then … then what? People are wonderfully surprised when they find that sexual relations are enjoyable and thrilling well into their eighties and beyond.

Life is equally thrilling in all its aspects, if we continue to focus on growth—that new page in the book—and not complacency.

In Figure 2.1, you can see that we have to make a "leap" as our growth slows. This applies to business growth and personal growth. The success trap lies in wait on the plateaus.

First, all plateaus will eventually erode because of the laws of entropy. If you don't bring new energy into a system, the system will exhaust the existing energy and then collapse.

Second, during dramatic growth, we have the momentum to make the leap (at the "x") to the next S-curve. However, if we plateau, that leap becomes far more difficult and has zero momentum.

So the issue becomes one of creating our own business growth, as entrepreneurs or employees, and our own personal growth as contributing and valuable individuals. This becomes somewhat more difficult—and therefore more urgent—if society tends to devalue you because of biases about age and competence.

Here's a brief test of your history and willingness to jump S-curves. Ask yourself:

1. When was the last time I tried to learn a new game or engage in a new sport?
2. How often do I express creativity and innovation in any form?
3. When did I last develop a new, rewarding, continuing friendship?
4. To what extent am I coaching or mentoring others?

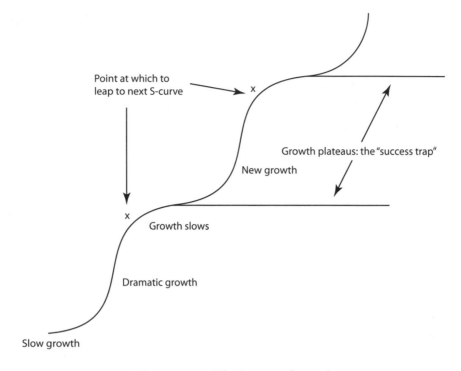

Point at which to
leap to next S-curve → x

Growth plateaus: the "success trap"

New growth

x
Growth slows

Dramatic growth

Slow growth

Figure 2.1 *The S-curve of growth.*

5. Am I producing ideas that others are embracing to improve their work and their lives?
6. Am I involved in the arts as a participant, observer, and/or patron?
7. To what extent am I involved in political and social causes beyond merely reading about them?
8. How often do people seek me out as an expert on any matter?

You don't need a scoring key. If the answers to these are mostly positive, your momentum is upward on the curve. If they are mostly negative, you're on the plateau. It's time to do something about that.

A train station is a stop along the route, intended to be brief. A train terminal is the end of the line, where the train can go no farther. We may occasionally find ourselves in a station but not getting off the train. Don't create a terminal before you have to.

A Legacy Is a Journey, Not an Ending

When my wife and I were first married, she was making $7000 a year as a public school teacher and I was making $7500 at Prudential Insurance as an assistant manager. Even in 1968–1969, that was not a lot of money.

On our first anniversary, we had no money in the bank and my wife asked what we should do about it.

"We should take a vacation," I announced firmly.

"And how would we do that?" she asked.

Well, they had just invented the MasterCard, and I was offered one with a credit limit of $350! (That's the kind of risk I was.) But I had found a vacation package offer on Marco Island in Florida that, for $350, got us airline tickets, 6 nights and 7 days in a hotel, all meals, and all beach amenities. So if I maxed out my card, we could go. (I figured I could pay it back at $10 per month for about 31 years.)

The vacation was just as promised; it was wonderful. On the beach, in the middle of the week, I told my wife I was going to take a small sailboat out.

"You've never sailed, you don't swim that well, is this a good idea?" she rhetorically inquired.

"For my $350, I'm using *every* beach amenity," I explained, and off I went.

Sure enough, about 100 yards off shore, I capsized. So I tread water, didn't panic, and yelled for help. And I yelled and I waved. And the guys running the sailboat concession waved back.

Finally, they realized I wasn't going to stop shouting, so they jumped into their powerboat and cruised out to me. The guy in front jumped in the water, walked over to me, turned the boat upright, put me back in it, and walked back to his boat.

Now there was a huge crowd on the beach, with my wife in the middle staring at the sky.

When you think the water is deep, you tread water. Perception IS reality.

And so I ask you, what is your perception of your life, your work, and the world around you? Are you reacting virtually, misguidedly, or accurately? Your legacy will be what others see, hear, and believe, not necessarily what you perceive it to be. So aligning your perceptions with the greater reality is critical for success.

Not long ago there was a survey of the customers of an advertising agency. It turned out that the customers *had a higher perception of the value of the ad agency than the agency personnel themselves believed the customers had*. Now, you might think that's wonderful, sort of like a bank error in your favor, but think harder. This firm's pricing, service, deliverables, and compromises (negotiations) were all based on the belief that the customer wasn't as happy with them as the customer really was. That was a significant business obstacle.

What are people thinking of you? Your legacy is formed daily.

I was once the CEO of a behavioral consulting firm. We used psychometric testing to unearth behavioral traits that were effective or ineffective for various jobs (e.g., you don't want to hire an unassertive salesperson or an unapproachable counselor). The power of the process is that we measured both how the individual saw himself or herself (ipsative) and how others viewed the person (normative).

When those two images were closely aligned, there was a feeling of "authenticity," as we hear it referred to today. Great trust was established quickly. But when the images were unaligned, there were problems and issues of dissonance because the individual viewed himself one way but others saw a different person. Hence, the person's expectation of being believed readily or hope for quick support did not materialize.

What is your alignment, and how does it affect your legacy? Consider these questions:

1. Do you sometimes receive surprising feedback that you automatically believe is a mistake on the other person's part?
2. Do you sometimes complain of not being understood or "read" correctly or that your remarks were misinterpreted?

3. Do you underestimate the time and energy required to influence others and to gain their support?
4. Do you receive compliments you feel are unearned or simply meant to make you feel good?
5. Do you become involved in debates and arguments that you didn't expect?
6. Do you find yourself having to take a lot of time to explain yourself?
7. Are you often subject to questions you didn't anticipate?

Positive answers to these questions indicate that your image of yourself and the one others have of you may be misaligned. Because you're writing that book page every day, it's important to change this now; otherwise, you'll find the book has an ending you never intended to write! (Or, worse, people will stop reading it.)

This is all a question of esteem, and our esteem too often suffers as we grow older. We're told without foundation or evidence that we're no longer on top of our game. We're told that people our age "no longer do that" (whether "that" is sports or sex). We're forced to let others take care of us (discounts, government services, prompts to go to the head of the line), and such treatment makes us unwittingly dependent.

The more dependent you are, the more your self-esteem suffers, and the more your self-esteem suffers, the more your efficacy suffers. And the more your efficacy suffers, the more dependent you are. You get the picture: It's a vicious circle.

Figure 2.2 shows another way to consider the relationship between self-esteem and efficacy. High self-esteem and high efficacy provide personal and professional health. The absence of both creates disaffection and alienation. High self-esteem without efficacy creates the "empty suit" we all mock (in Texas, "big hat, no cattle"). *And high efficacy but low self-esteem presents the condition that too many people allow to plague them: the imposter syndrome.*

We have to continually build our self-esteem to create a legacy of health. The virtuous circle is that autonomy begets high self-esteem, which creates high efficacy, which promotes autonomy.

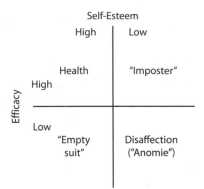

Figure 2.2 *Self-esteem and efficacy.*

That's the true circle of life at any age.

You *Can* Make Up Lost Ground

As I noted earlier, it's silly to wait until the day you want to sell your business to increase its value for prospective buyers. It's poor planning to try to enhance your corporate performance the day before a promotion decision. It's ridiculous to try to create a particular lasting impression for others on your deathbed. And it's insane to think that you can change your relationship with your kids on the eve of a divorce, departure, or new marriage.

Are we all in agreement here? The last minute doesn't work. If you're running a distance race, you can't make up a 50-yard gap in the final 10 yards. People tailgate on the highway going 70 miles per hour within 20 feet of the car ahead of them, relying on their own reflexes if they need to stop. But by the immutable laws of physics, by the time you see the red taillight illuminate, it's too late to stop, no matter how lightning quick you believe your reflexes to be. You'll be just as dead as if you had slower reflexes.

And as you read this, a great many people—maybe you're one of them and, if not, you certainly know a few—have woefully insufficient financial resources and are thinking that they have plenty of time to fix that, though they have not been able to thus far. About 46 percent of those who are officially "retired" die with less than $10,000 in the bank.[1] If that fact doesn't shake up such thinking, what will?

No matter who you are or where you are, you can make up for lost ground with your career, family, finances, and self-worth. My message here isn't "There's no hope" but rather "We need to do something more than just hope!"

The first and most important mental set is to not look back. We establish our course looking out the windshield, not at our wake, not in our rearview mirror. Sure, we could all have done things differently, but there's no changing that now. It's not water under the bridge, it's water that's evaporated. The indelible indicators of this rearward mentality are refrains like "I should have done this," "I wish I had said that," "I'd love to have the time to do that over." Instead of the "shouldas," as I call them, use your regrets as opportunities for learning, not remorse.[2]

The second dimension is control, which is the theme of this book. Stop bemoaning the feeling (not fact) that you have no control.

As Figure 2.3 shows, the healthiest mental set acknowledges external control (weather, laws, company rules) and its reciprocity with personal (internal) control (judgment, decisions, talent, and so forth). Winston Churchill said, "We shape our buildings, and afterwards, our buildings shape us," referring to Parliament. The fact is that we are impacted by the world and, in turn, impact it.

To think there are no controls at all means that every day consists of merely a random, meaningless wandering. To believe that there is only external control and you, yourself, have none is a kind of Calvinistic predestination that maintains it's hopeless to try to influence your fate. And the misguided belief—from motivational speakers, affirmations, and books such as *The Secret*—that if you think it, you can do it creates false trust and, basically, is a display of arrogance.

Confidence is the honest-to-God belief that you can help other people.

Arrogance is the honest-to-God belief that you have nothing left to learn yourself.

Smugness is arrogance without the talent.

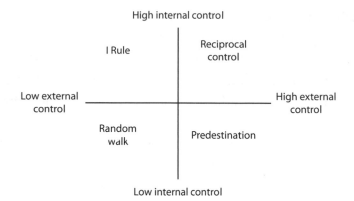

Figure 2.3   *Locus of control.*

To summarize, in terms of making up for lost chances and lost ground:

1. Look forward, not back, and make positive changes to create the person you want to be.
2. Understand that you have significant control, both over your own life and in the world around you.

Thus, here are some guidelines I suggest to instantly—*now*, not tomorrow, not when you get around to it, not when you finish other priorities—reroute your life and career so that your legacy is what you intend and each new page is different, exciting, and powerful.

1. **Consider changing your habits.** You're in whatever rut you're in because you consistently reinforce them, consciously or unconsciously. Take a different means or route to work. Redecorate your office. Change your technology setup. Call your kids instead of waiting for them to call you.
2. **Develop new friends.** In your social, civic, and recreational involvement, cultivate some people with whom you can share a dinner or a show. They may not all be candidates for further ventures, but some will be.

3. **Change your work.** If you're in an organization, ask for a transfer, seek a promotion, change your routine. If you're an entrepreneur, enter a new market, offer different value, "fire" unproductive and troublesome customers.

4. **Alter your family relationships.** Take more vacations, of differing durations, to new places. The vacation rut can be horrible if you only go to the same places at the same time every year. Spend the holidays away. Invite family over for no special reason. Reduce the amount of time you spend with consistently negative family members.

5. **Alter your lifelong learning.** Take a nonmatriculated course. Find a new hobby or interest (music, art, travel). Follow a new sport. Start reading books in genres new to you. Subscribe to different publications and unsubscribe to some existing ones. Learn other people's points of view. (As F. Scott Fitzgerald put it, "The test of a first-rate intelligence is the ability to hold two opposed ideas in the mind at the same time, and still retain the ability to function."[3])

You can't afford to let today be your future. Get help in changing if you need it. If you've been trying to change something unsuccessfully for many months, why do you think you can suddenly do so now? You obviously need help to make the move.

The Future Is Not a Different Version of Today

One of the biggest mistakes we make is to assume that the future is an extension of today (and that's why that page we're writing keeps looking the same). We tend to see ourselves like that insect captured in amber from a million years ago. It may be true that alligators and cockroaches haven't changed in millennia, but we're neither reptiles nor insects.

Moreover, we're self-aware, sentient. A tulip and a cheetah will grow to be tulips and cheetahs. But we have significant variation in our physical appearance, learning ability, personalities, emotions, and so forth. If you stand next to an elm tree, you don't begin to resemble an elm. (Some people say we grow to resemble our dogs or vice versa.) But you will resemble your parents or key nurturers in their habits and preferences as you mature. As a matter of fact, too many people become dentists or lawyers just because their parents were in those professions, despite the fact their own passions and skills lie elsewhere. They turn out to be very unhappy.

In observing my white German Shepherds over the years, I find the following:

- **Species commonality.** They are dogs and act like dogs, with a superb sense of smell, the need to mark territory, and so forth.
- **Breed commonality.** They are great with children, will defend you with their lives, and are working dogs requiring great exercise.
- **Dog-specific traits.** Koufax was aloof and wouldn't chase anything thrown. Bentley loves interaction constantly and is a champion Frisbee® player.

You may feel that you change ever so slightly each day and are only marginally different from others, all of whom eat, sleep, work, and so forth. You may feel that as a woman or a man you are indeed unique, or that at your age you're different, or that your geography makes a difference in who you are. Finally, you are probably aware of your individual difference in terms of hobbies, talents, relationships, and so on.

So far, however, you're not much different from my German Shepherds.

You're not an insect in amber, nor are you in a snapshot of your life; you're in a film. The frames are rushing by. The time you spent reading these last two pages will never return. If you hear nothing else, hear this: *You can always make another dollar, but you can never make another minute.*

Your future is what you decide it to be right now, not when you get around to it, and not when you attend some meeting on self-worth and personal goals conducted by someone whose own personal goals are to fill a room and make money by doing so.

Therefore, your future cannot be allowed to simply be a small variation of today. The life you're currently leading is not your future life. That sounds like what I call an "obviousity," but it's far more profound. If you think about the control issues we've discussed previously, I'm talking about constant growth and change, and *the acquisition of power and leverage, not its sacrifice.*

The "good old days" usually refer to a fictional time when we feel we were better off because we think we had more control. But those are inaccurate recollections. We're really bemoaning the fact that we feel powerless today. Most organizations' largest expense is people, and the greatest monetary loss comes from their absence and disability—and the cause of that absence is primarily stress. The two greatest causes of stress are the belief that one doesn't know what's going to happen tomorrow and the belief that one can't influence what will happen, in any event.[4]

The future, starting tonight or tomorrow, *will be a different version of today*, not the same. Thus, the question becomes, What are you going to do to create the future most beneficial to you?

One problem we face as we age arises from a phenomenon I've coined "nesting syndrome." This occurs at work and at home when we've mistakenly focused on becoming comfortable rather than creating challenges and excitement for ourselves. It arises when we place comfort before growth.

Below are the categories. Ask yourself whether the statements following each category describe you today.

Nesting Syndrome

- **Unconscious competency.** We do things on autopilot and have insufficient self-awareness, oblivious to opportunities around us. We need to retreat to conscious competency.
- **Refusal to shake things up.** We conspire to allow things that are working to continue, instead of proactively searching for better ways. "If it ain't broke, fix it anyway" should be our philosophy.

- **Failure to create new value.** In business, we don't think to provide new value to our best customers. Socially, we don't provide it to our friends and colleagues. And with our life partner, we don't provide new intimacy.
- **Failure to solicit referrals.** We neglect to ask our customers and clients to introduce us to prospects, provide testimonials, or serve as references. We think we'd be inconveniencing them, so we don't disturb the nest.
- **"King of the Hill" deception.** Because we're so comfortable and happy, we're seldom challenged. Our kids think we've got it made. Others point to us as exemplars. But the reality is that when we're not challenged, we're not growing. Top companies with no close competition create routes to raise their own bars. So should we all.
- **Problem-solving without innovation.** We fix things quickly and efficiently, but we neglect to raise the bar, as alluded to previously. We don't think innovatively, only in terms of the nest we're occupying.
- **Avoidance of sharp right turns (Figure 2.4).** Reinvention shouldn't be subtle or gradual. There comes a point at which we should abandon the S-curves of growth and make a sharp right turn to create a number-one presence in a completely new direction.[5]
- **Refusal to fire clients and friends.** As mentioned, some friends we can't and shouldn't keep forever. They represent the friendships we had when we were different people. They only help feather the same nest. I also recommend dropping the bottom 15 percent of your clients in profit each year or so, because they are using up more time than they're worth. Harsh, but true.
- **Chasing money.** We chase the wrong clients and the wrong opportunities under the illusion that we have the time and there's money on the table. This is false. You can't make more time, so make your money only where there is an excellent chance for success and you're doing something you love and are great at. *Never assume that your calling is to make money whenever and wherever possible.*

Figure 2.4 *The sharp right turn.*

- **Low intellectual property (IP) generation.** In business, you need to be generating new ideas and approaches, especially as an entrepreneur. In your own life, you need to be creative in your recreation, family relationships, personal growth, and so forth. Otherwise, you're just sitting in the nest waiting for death.
- **Sharing the nest with the wrong species.** You need to coexist with people who stretch you, not merely dependents and not solely peers. If those people won't visit your nest, you have to go to theirs.
- **Not failing enough.** If you're not failing, in life and work, you're simply not trying hard enough. Avoiding failure is not a calling, it's a statement about insecurity and the false sense of the need for perfection. Life isn't perfect, and nests aren't waterproof or impregnable; get used to it.
- **Fear of flying.** Stay in the nest long enough and you become fearful that you've forgotten how to fly. So you settle in deeper and wait for the end.

How many of these statements describe you? Remember, the future is a lot more than a different version of today.

Let's examine how you can use your power to create that future.

Notables

Diana Nyad, 64. Became the first person to swim from Cuba to Florida.
Audrey Crabtree, 99. Finished her high school diploma.

Noriko Shinohara, 59. Successful artist (as is her husband, Ushio, 81).
Dr. Ruth Westheimer, 85. Expert on sexual relationships.
John Mahoney, 73. Achieved highest stardom as an actor (*Frasier*).
Estelle Getty, 81. Finally achieved acting acclaim (*Golden Girls*).
Kathryn Bigelow, 61. Became first woman to win an Oscar as a director.
Taikichiro Mori, 88. Realtor worth twice as much as Bill Gates.
Miguel de Cervantes, 68. Published *Don Quixote*.

Notes

1. Marie Backman, "Almost Half of Americans Die Broke," *USA Today*, June 2, 2017, https://www.usatoday.com/story/money/personalfinance/retirement/2017/06/02/almost-half-of-americans-die-nearly-broke/102312340/.
2. If you'd like to learn about the "should haves" and their basis in depth: Karen Horney, *Neurosis and Human Growth*, W.W. Norton, New York, 1950.
3. F. Scott Fitzgerald, "The Crack-Up," *Esquire*, February 1936.
4. American Institute of Stress, "Workplace Stress," 2017, https://www.stress.org/workplace-stress/.
5. When Calgon was a distant number three in the water treatment business, I helped them become number one instantly in the "effluent management" business we created.

CHAPTER 3

Power Increases with Age

The image of grandparents sacrificing their own lives to take care of their grandchildren while their children hold down two jobs (or simply take vacations) has to be smashed. Age does not suggest involuntary servitude (based on guilt), nor the obligation to make your children wealthy from your own assets. Power actually increases with age, and we might as well feel free about that and get good at applying it.

Maximizing and Utilizing Travel and Experiences

Part of the power of aging is in the irreplaceable experiences derived along the journey. That's why people in their twenties should be reading this, because we often sacrifice opportunities to experience things while we're young. I've established that you can make up for lost ground, but there's only so much you can cram into life over 50 if you've lived like a hermit before that.

We all scoff at job descriptions and recruitment ads that require 5 years of experience, knowing full well that experience is *qualitative* not *quantitative.* By that I mean: 5 years of mediocre experience or the same 1 year of good experience merely repeated mean virtually nothing except that the person hasn't grown.

Circumscribed experience is also the problem with those who return, like nesting geese, to the same vacation habitats year in and year out. There's nothing wrong with a favorite place (hell, we've been going to Nantucket, AKA God's Country, for 25 consecutive years), but we've also visited the Jersey shore, Japan, Fiji, Iceland, Italy, and so on—about 60 countries over the years.

We need a conscious strategy to build our experiences and travel opportunities. When I was in my early thirties, my wife and I bid a tearful goodbye to both sets of parents in New Jersey and headed out to San Francisco, where I was to run the local office of the consulting firm that employed me for 2 years. The owner of the company said, "I can't think of two people who will make more of this opportunity than you and Maria." After huge success there, I ran the Far East and South American operations (I calculated 36 million square miles of ocean in my domain) while living back east once again.

We saw the world.

But in so doing, I also achieved more than any MBA degree could ever provide. I managed people, fired people, hired people; I dealt with customers and romanced prospects; I managed finances, publicity, and marketing; I dealt with building maintenance and civic responsibilities; and I was responsible to a home office 3000 miles yonder.

It was at about age 40 that I was recruited to be president of another firm and, having been fired from that job, equipped myself to run my own practice. Today, I have the strongest brand in solo consulting in the world and have written more books about consulting than anyone, ever.

I'm not advocating that you engage in foreign responsibilities for your company, only that—no matter what your stage of life—you maximize your experiences. The rubric is that organizations tend to fire older, higher-paid workers and replace them with younger, less expensive workers. But no company I know of that thrives fires *valuable* workers. Recall that Atlantic Electric example I mentioned earlier. Transfer the labor of rigging power lines in ice storms to the mental acuity needed to deal with customer problems, anticipate new market needs, and innovate to gain market share.

Or think of it in terms of invaluable customer service, the distinctive training of others, or superb community service. We can all make ourselves irreplaceable if we build a personal experiential base and are unafraid to stand out in a crowd.

When organizations "downsize" (how I hate that euphemism), for every one person released, they lose three other people:

- The person who feels guilty it wasn't him or her and whose performance declines
- The person who hides under the desk and disconnects the phone so he or she is hard to find
- The person who is superb and untouchable who decides to get a résumé out on the street because of what's going on

You can be that third person if you aren't simply one of the "crowd." Your "travels" (experience) will set you apart.

People are loath to take on new jobs or responsibilities because they fear failure. Yet the real failure is in not taking on new responsibilities that single you out. Here's an observation from Meng Tzu (Mencius), dating to about 2500 years ago:

To act without knowing why; to do things as they have always been done, without asking why; to engage in an activity all one's life without really understanding what it is about and how it relates to other things—this is to be one of the crowd.

Obviously, I'm not introducing a new concept, just one that's not regularly observed. Think about your colleagues, friends, and family members. Do any stand out as leading exceptional lives and thriving? Why is that?

Barring an intelligently invested inheritance from Great Aunt Matilda, it's because they have lived—and are living—a life of experiences, travels, and prudent risk. This means we have to be healthily selfish.

I've coached people to apply what I've coined the "oxygen mask principle." Every single time we fly we hear the admonition, "Place your own oxygen mask on first before attempting to help those around you." The reason is that if you die, you can't help anyone; it's as simple as that. And that's why sacrificing your life for your children makes no sense. I'm not talking about kidney transplants but rather watching the kids daily so that your daughter and son-in-law can both hold down full-time jobs. In so doing, we enable poor choices and we deny ourselves our lives. We need the oxygen of a full life, not one of guardianship.

I've known many couples who pay for child care that is about equal in cost to one of the spouse's salaries, so it's a wash. I know work is fulfilling, but so is raising a child, right?

No matter your age, whether at work or at play, you must gather and exploit the available experiences that will make you a more valuable person, an object of interest, irreplaceable—despite the number of years you've occupied the Earth. The Great Wall of China can't really be appreciated, despite any digital medium, without walking on it and understanding the sheer magnificence of the project conceived eons ago. The Pietà, the David, The Night Watch, and Victoria Falls are not truly represented by media, only by experience.

You don't learn to ride a bike or ski by reading a book. You learn by doing and then teaching someone else. You can't create a meaningful and valuable life by reading about the exploits of others or by watching them on a computer or by imagining them.

You have to travel outside the shadow of your own existence and into the reality of the world around you. It's your choice whether you see a world in black and white or in living color.

Improving and Expanding Language

There are four basic communication dynamics that can make you stand out or shrink back.

1. To speak with influence
2. To write with expression

3. To listen with discernment
4. To read with comprehension

All of these are dependent on verbal skills, either written or oral ("verbal" refers to language, not solely spoken language, so there's lesson one).

The ability to use language correctly and to "decipher" language is a critical element of not just retaining power but of *building* power. We can readily build our vocabularies and comprehension skills as we age. There is no direct and immutable connection between aging and brain power (as there is, for example, with lung capacity or muscle tone). Just as we can work out to improve our stamina and strength, we can mentally "work out" to improve—not merely maintain—our linguistic skills.

Think about who most influences you in speaking or writing. They are people with a command of language. They use language economically (they are not verbose—Lincoln delivered the Gettysburg Address in about 2 minutes or so). They use language colorfully ("I have a dream…" "A city upon a hill…" "Ask not what your country can do for you…"). And they tell finely honed stories.

Here's a quick quiz: Provide the definitions for the 12 words below. They appear in casual English, in that they are not scientific or technical terms. The answers are at the end of this section.

- Recondite
- Phlegmatic
- Circumspect
- Invidious
- Manifold
- Panoply
- Derivative
- Equanimity
- Mnemonic
- Schism
- Chimera
- Effervescent

Most people I've tried this with can roughly identify about four of these words. My belief is that you should know all of them.

If you want to impress business colleagues, clients, prospects, friends, suppliers, subcontractors—anyone—you must learn to use language *powerfully*. The difference in having recommendations accepted, applying influence effectively, winning a debate, negotiating terms, reconciling conflict, coaching others, and building a personal (or business) brand is immense.

Language is one of our key tools for exerting more and more power as we mature.

Here are my suggestions for building your verbal chops and becoming a force in your daily interactions, every one of which—from reading newspapers to participating in meetings, from hiring help to closing new business—relies heavily on influence, expression, discernment, and comprehension.

Begin a word file. Throughout my life, when I encountered a word I didn't know, I wrote it on an index card, looked up the definition, and then used it as soon as I could. I still have the file boxes. However, when I first started, I had to write the word, get a dictionary, file the card, and review it. Today, you can immediately look a word up online and keep an electronic file with words and definitions that are easy to review. Originally, I would look up two words a week or more. Today, I look up perhaps one a month or fewer.

Here are the discernments you can make, depending on the situation in which you find yourself. I'm not talking about super-elegant speech or oratory; but just as my father-in-law would tell me that you need the right tool to do the right job, you need the right word to create the right influence.

All three words below mean essentially the same thing: "a confused mixture."

- **Basic speech:** Hodgepodge
- **Fluent speech:** Farrago
- **Sophisticated speech:** Gallimaufry

If you use the word "hodgepodge" with me at a bar, it's entirely appropriate. If we're at a meeting with investors, you might use "farrago." And if you're with the trustees of a private school you can use "gallimaufry." Let me infer here that you're thinking some of this is over the top. But "over the top" is where you want to be, looking down at others, not "at the bottom" staring up, especially as you age.

I recall making a visit to a banking prospect who actually looked up a word as I was speaking. (I had used "adverse" in my comments.) He was learning too. I got the assignment.

The advice to dumb down your speech (or your dress) is about the worst I've ever encountered and usually emanates from people who themselves feel they can't perform at a higher level and want to bring everyone else to their own perceived level of ineptitude. The best teachers and professors address the upper third of the class, demanding that everyone else stretch and run to catch up, rather than hobbling and slowing down the top performers.

So, I ask you, do you want to be perceived as among the top performers or as someone racing to catch up as you grow older?

Here are key tools to employ and to observe in both spoken and written language. In addition to your word list, try adding these techniques to your communications. They are the spices that create a memorable meal.

- **Metaphor.** That's my oxygen mask principle, comparing two disparate things that actually have something in common that's highly relevant.
- **Alliteration.** The repeated use of an initial consonant: fighting fate's fickleness.
- **Hyperbole.** Extravagance to make a point: "You couldn't catch him with a cheetah."
- **Litotes.** Profound understatement, as in "Meryl Streep isn't a bad actor."
- **Metonymy.** Substituting something nearby or associated with the actual thing, as in "The White House issued a release today," though it was actually the press secretary who did it.
- **Simile.** The classic figure of speech, using "as" or "like" to make comparisons between dissimilar things, such as "He ran the race like prey trying to escape a predator."

- **Synecdoche.** Substituting a part for the whole, as in "Germany won the World Cup" when it was actually a single team from that country.

If a picture is worth a thousand words, the proper figures of speech are worth a thousand pictures.

Definitions

- **Recondite.** Little known, abstruse
- **Phlegmatic.** Unemotional and calm
- **Circumspect.** Wary and risk averse
- **Invidious.** Unjust, likely to incur anger
- **Manifold.** Numerous and various[2]
- **Panoply.** A complete and impressive display
- **Derivative.** Based on other work
- **Equanimity.** Composure and calmness
- **Mnemonic.** A pattern that assists memory
- **Schism.** A split or division
- **Chimera.** Something illusory, not real
- **Effervescent.** Giving off bubbles (or enthusiastic)

Knowledge Is for Kids: Creating Wisdom

Wisdom is historically associated with the mature. Why do we tend to give up that connection? Because it is often assumed, and we sacrifice the power by not exhibiting wisdom.

Let's begin with the proper sequence:

- **Data.** Facts and statistics available for examination and analysis. We may have data about the attrition rate in the company or mileage between geographic points.

- **Information.** Collections of data that constitute *learning*. We use the collection of data to understand that our attrition rate is worse than the industry average or that there is construction and thus delays along the route we seek to travel.
- **Knowledge.** That synergy of information, talents, and skills acquired through experience and education. We know that our attrition rate is hurting profits and how to improve it, and that there are alternate routes that, while longer, will be faster. Knowledge often refers to a particular field or endeavor, and we may be knowledgeable about music but uninformed about mathematics.
- **Wisdom.** The quality of having the appropriate knowledge, judgment, experience, and perspective to make excellent decisions and accurate predictions, and to serve as an expert for others. We realize that people leave managers, not companies, and make it a point to hire and promote managers with the retention of talent in mind, not based solely on their past performance. We create a Plan B and even Plan C for our travels, knowing that there are variables outside our control that can't be prevented but can be ameliorated.

We're surrounded by data, especially in the digital age. We have so much, we don't know what to do with it all. Information is at our fingertips. As I write this, if I need a source or supporting details, I can immediately access them on the internet, but I can also simply ask Alexa to respond aloud (I just Googled how to spell "Alexa").

In school, we once had to regurgitate information to earn our grades: the year of the French Revolution, the formula used to calculate the square footage of a roof, the countries bordering the Mediterranean Sea. But that type of recitation is useless today because all that information is on our mobile devices and accessible within seconds. Why memorize it?

Building knowledge took some time, some annealing of disparate elements as we worked, traveled, experienced life. Supposedly, companies look for knowledge among those who they hire and promote. We have some people, almost savants, who have great knowledge in one area (football coach

Vince Lombardi, Apple founder Steve Jobs) but are almost incompetent in most others. Knowledge isn't universally pragmatic.

But as we mature, wisdom is possible (though far from automatic). We hear about street smarts, but our reference for wisdom is "wise guys," which is pejorative at best and refers to criminals at worst. We've chosen owls as representative of the wise, yet they are murderous hunters that only operate nocturnally.

Wisdom needs to be exhibited and proclaimed. It's a huge benefit of maturity (no one is expecting 25-year-olds to be wise, which is why people say "wise beyond their years"). Here's why:

- **People tend to follow and heed those deemed wise.** Examples include Warren Buffet in investments, Bill Belichick in football, Michael Tilson Thomas in music, Walter Cronkite in news, Norman Lear in entertainment, Henry Kissinger in government, Peter Drucker in business. What they say and initiate is carefully considered and usually accepted. The same occurs on a smaller scale in business and the community.

- **Wisdom becomes the center of attention.** Have you seen people who immediately command a room? All attention turns to them. It's often attributed to their charisma and/or communications ability (see our discussion above), and rightly so. But it's often a connection achieved because people feel wisdom, like luck, can be shared through osmosis, through association. My friend and colleague, über-coach Marshall Goldsmith, said once, "The way to become a thought leader is to hang out with thought leaders." (He hung out with Peter Drucker.)

- **Wisdom is imbued with power.** People flock to power. People who are seen as wise will make predictions that are more accepted than challenged, and that support actually enables the prediction to come true (just look at the stock market), which enhances the verity of future predictions.

- **Wisdom is eternal: It never goes out of style.** We still quote Aristotle and Socrates. We may hear, "We won't miss her, there are a lot of smart people to take her place," or, "He can go, his knowledge in the field isn't unique or irreplaceable." But people don't say, "Don't worry, we can easily replace their wisdom." That's because wisdom isn't something you get out of a book or by treading on hot coals. It's something that accrues with the experiences and education that come with age *if you're willing to identify that trait and apply it shamelessly.*

Here are my suggestions for using the leverage of wisdom to separate yourself from the crowd and magnify your presence, create a great career, and become indispensable.

1. Formally identify the experiences you have acquired that constitute uniqueness. Where have you traveled? Who have you managed? What positions have you accepted? What health issues have you experienced and overcome or accepted? Who have you coached? What did you correctly anticipate? (Did you buy Apple stock at $17?) What have you successfully recovered from? (Did you triumph after being fired?)
2. Formally identify what your *informal* education has told you. How do people tend to act under what conditions? How are the best people influenced? When and why will they change positions? For example: You can only help people who want to be helped. What does that mean for business and friends?
3. Manifest your wisdom. You don't need to ascend a mountain or set up a crystal ball. You simply need to be unafraid to comment. Experts make predictions. Thought leaders are willing to communicate provocative positions and new ideas. You can't hold back. No one recognizes unspoken wisdom. The power of threescore and more is in blowing your own horn—because if you don't, *there is no music.*

Let's look at how that's done.

A Story about Stories

I was addressing a senior group of editors at the American Press Institute. I told them everyone has a story that gives them a claim to wisdom. One woman said, "I have no story." Here's what followed:

"Where did you go to school?"
"West Point."
"West Point!? You must have been in an early class of women who were accepted."
"I was in the first class of women."
"How did you do?"
"Well, I became brigade commander."
"You were the highest ranking student after 4 years?"
"Yes, but then I simply entered the army."
"What did you do there?"
"I was a paratrooper."
"And you have no story?!"
Today, she's a Carmelite nun.
Everyone has a story; sometimes we need help realizing it.

The Value of Healthy Selfishness and Comfort

The oxygen mask principle noted above demands that, for greater safety, you take care of yourself first. I wouldn't want a flight attendant and pilot sacrificing their oxygen, because they're in a position to save everyone.

Yet, as individuals, as organizations, and as a society, we tend to make inappropriate sacrifices, which multiply to harm rather than help others.

Simple acts of generosity, humility, or donation can rebound to cause great pain and suffering if we don't think them through, or if we make them out of an overarching (and false) sense of guilt and atonement.

For example, a great deal of foreign aid from the United States to drought-stricken countries kills local agriculture and has far more damaging and long-lasting adverse effects than the condition we're attempting to ameliorate. By supplying thousands of tons of free food, we undermine the need for local farmers' crops, causing their enterprises to fail and eliminating the farm industry. When the drought ends, the country is totally dependent on foreign aid (which will probably never stop) because its food infrastructure has been destroyed.

We meant well, but we didn't think sufficiently ahead for long-term gain. We felt our sacrifice (of food, money, workers) was sufficient.

The same principle dogs us as we mature, have children, and eventually wind up acting as parents to the people who are actually our parents as they decline in old age or illness. On a business level, we hear about "taking a hit for the team," an athletic term meaning that a player has made a sacrifice, often resulting in injury, for the good of all. (The bunt, in baseball, where a batter will probably be thrown out in order to advance another base runner, is referred to as a "sacrifice.") People once worshipped gods by offering sacrifices of animals that they really couldn't afford to lose. One wonders if any ancient sociologists studied those who made sacrifices and those who didn't in a longitudinal study to examine whether their lives turned out any differently! (Or perhaps the social scientists of the time were busy making their own sacrifices.)

Healthy selfishness refers to taking care of yourself without guilt or blame. Guilt is that quality of believing you have been responsible for some offense or crime. It's become a neologism, a distorted verb: "She was guilted into volunteering her time for the fundraiser." "Blame" assigns accountability for wrongdoings, errors, and sins. Guilt, like clinical depression, masks talents and undermines energy and initiative. We hear people talk about the "blame game" in both business and families.

How can we avoid the false humility and misconceived arrogance that undermine us? Here's an example of looking at such factors empirically (as they should have looked at those animal sacrifices and their actual utility):

Many coaches, especially life coaches, I've encountered are quite good at helping people. They are sincere, competent, and don't charge as much as they should. They don't make as much money as they should (not "could" but "should") because they feel it's arrogant to self-promote. Instead, they sit at home and wait for prospects to call them because they believe their reputation and results are so strong and so constantly mentioned that people will call them.

Sitting by that phone waiting for people to come to you is arrogant. Telling people assertively that you can help them because you know you can and they need you is not arrogant, it's being of service.[1]

Do you see the irony here? These professionals have mixed up "arrogance" so that they underperform. Imagine if the flight attendant felt that using her own oxygen mask first, or giving others directions, was arrogant?

Believing you can help people is not arrogant, *nor is the condition that you have to feel good about yourself and help yourself in order to best do so.*

A personal story: My wife and I dine out every night. One night, I told her we couldn't leave home until 8:00 p.m., though we generally left at 6:00 p.m. She was puzzled, but then a car carrier backed down our long driveway with a single car on top. The driver carefully off-loaded it and my wife exclaimed, "My God, you bought the Ferrari! Alan, with our tuition payments (both kids in college at $50,000 per semester at the time) is this really prudent?"

I said, "Maria, this is my way of not resenting the tuition payments." And, indeed, I paid for private education for both my kids for 17 years each, in addition to the 60 percent of my local taxes going to support public schools that we never used, *and* made my exotic car payments.

You might feel buying that car was selfish or imprudent, but I knew, for me, it was an important motivator. Yet you and I both know people who constantly sacrifice until some event that will never end will be "over." Those sacrifices undermine you. Helping yourself makes helping others easier.

Here's how to have the attitude that enables you to take care of yourself guilt-free and offer even better support to others:

Doing things for yourself and for others is not mutually exclusive. Don't automatically put yourself second; put yourself first, when possible. If your spouse wants you at a fundraiser, and you had plans to golf, suggest you move your golf date earlier in the day and that you arrive at the fundraiser after it begins but before the fundraising auction.

- Stop being a child to your parents. Your parents are quite capable of unreasonable requests. If your parents insist that you drive them to the airport whenever they take a trip, and it's not convenient or sensible, simply offer to pay for a car to pick them up. Being an unhappy chauffeur does not prove your love for them.
- If a colleague at work says that the project won't be completed because, even though he has responsibility for this segment, your expertise is important to access and you should stay late with him, tell him (don't suggest, tell) that you'll be accessible by email that evening but you have an agreement to watch the ball game with your son.
- When your kids desire something expensive that was unplanned and is not critical, ask them how they intend to contribute toward the purchase.
- When the car dealer says that they need your car an extra day because they underestimated the repair time and you have appointments the next day, tell them to send over a loaner.
- Finally, learn to simply say no *without justification*. If you're asked why you can't attend, or support, or act, simply say you choose not to at the moment. Once you provide some excuse, people will find away around it ("Well, then, why don't you escort next week's trip instead of this week's?").

The lesson here, to retain power and control, is *Don't enable the people who are requiring the subordination of your objectives in order to meet theirs*. People tend to believe that, as we mature, our time isn't as important.

Au contraire, it's more important than ever. I can't repeat this enough: *You can always make another dollar, but you can never make another minute.*

Notables

Will and Ariel Durant, 90 and 81. Completed *The Story of Civilization.*

Alfred Lunt and Lynne Fontanne, 72 and 67. Received the Presidential Medal of Freedom.

George Burns, 79. Won the Academy Award for Best Supporting Actor; at 99, signed a 10-year contract to perform in Las Vegas.

Mick Jagger, 75. On tour, still lead man for the Rolling Stones.

Aretha Franklin, 75. Still performing, brought down the house at the 2016 Kennedy Center Awards.

Raúl Castro, 86. President of Cuba.

Elizabeth II, 91. Queen of England.

Jorge Mario Bergoglio (Francis), 80. Pope.

Roger Penske, 80. Chairman, Penske Automotive Group.

Notes

1. An issue for a different book is that most of these undercharging and nonassertive marketers are female.
2. This is also a part of an internal combustion engine.

CHAPTER 4

Biceps, Quads, and
Self-Esteem Are All Muscles

As we age, we tend to look in all the wrong places for validation—our friends, our children, our spouses. That is a surrender of basic power and potential. Older people work out in gyms, ride bikes, run, play tennis, and so forth. So, too, should they work on their self-esteem and mental well-being. We are not what the media, advertisers, young people, or the government tells us. We are who we are (I am who I am), which has worked for both Popeye and God.

Daily Workouts on Self-Worth

Nearly 20 percent of Americans 65 or above are working or seeking work, the highest percentage since 1962.[1] Traditional pension plans have largely vanished. Social security was intended, from its outset, only as a supplement to retirement income, extended family support, and part-time work. Personal savings have seriously declined in a profligate world where interest rates on traditional investments are at historic lows. (In some countries, such as Germany, you actually pay a fee to have money in your accounts in the banks.)

The number of private sector employees in traditional pension plans that have incentives to retire at certain ages has steadily declined to under 15 percent.[2] I could go on. Yet the primary reason that older people and those at traditional retirement ages remain in the workforce is not economic deprivation but rather a need to work in a culture that respects work and contributions. In addition, the medical community has identified continued work and involvement as important for ongoing mental acuity.[3]

Having acknowledged that maturing people continue to work because of financial needs in some cases and family needs in others (e.g., helping children pay off educational loans, helping parents in assisted living facilities), I contend that the vast preponderance of people *actively desire to keep working to feel productive, involved, and vibrant.* Remember, we grow older because we *stop* playing.

In order to remain effective in jobs, careers, volunteer work, coaching, and other pursuits, we need to maximize our own perceptions of our self-worth. Let's begin with some of my definitions:

- **Efficacy.** The ability to do something well, whether that is playing a musical instrument, managing people, or investing funds.
- **Self-esteem.** The daily sense that you are competent and effective, despite setbacks. I consider self-esteem a muscle that, no different from biceps or quads, has to be exercised and properly challenged so it won't atrophy. Another way to regard it is as a verb, an active tense in your life. I equate this with the term "self-worth." In other words, no matter how inefficacious you are in certain pursuits, your own worth doesn't suffer. Failing doesn't make you a bad person. A sales rejection doesn't undermine you and a personal rejection doesn't stun you. You don't question your own validity.
- **Self-confidence.** This is the noun to self-esteem's verb. It is a condition you reach wherein you have absolute trust in your talents, traits, abilities, and judgment. You are almost never thrown off the horse; you can ride in any terrain.

Our daily workout in self-esteem, our trip to the mental and emotional gym, has to include an understanding of the following facts:

- Our contributions and abilities don't decline with age. I know that we can't run as fast or jump as high, but we can think as clearly and with recourse to more experience. We can be wise and use judgment well. Our contributions are not merely physical; in fact, that's the least of it. We need to see ourselves as contributing individuals, holistically.

- We are individuals, not clones within some arbitrary cohort of generations, as described at the outset of this book. We may see people around us declining, just as we see people in their twenties who have stopped growing. That condemns neither those in their twenties nor those in their sixties.
- We have to resist the normative pressures to "act our age." We're stereotyped by others. The senior partners in the firm are "figureheads." The people close to mandatory retirement are "lame ducks." These people are taking the place—hogging the jobs—of younger people who seek to advance. This job requires more energy than they can provide. This is all hokum. Do you want the best heart surgeon around, or only one under fifty? Do you want to listen to a cellist under 40 or Yo-Yo Ma?
- "Seniors competitions" (golf, tennis, track and field, marathons) are meant to provide outlets that accommodate the inevitable physical changes that accompany aging. However, there are no seniors competitions for investment experts, attorneys, salespeople, insurance underwriters, coaches, architects, or store owners. Don't confuse inevitable physical limitations with mental abilities.

Perhaps one of the greatest and most referenced disparagements of people maturing at work came in the form of the character Willy Loman, created by Arthur Miller in his play *Death of a Salesman*. The notion that older people can't adjust, can't accept feedback, and are stuck in their ways made for a sensational fictional production but not a factual documentary of our time.

I'm not going to suggest what you hear all the time: Do crossword puzzles and word games, read more, write letters, and so forth. These are well-meaning devices for mental activity that, while helpful, carry the baggage of being intended for the feeble.

My advice is to keep working, with financial support being a by-product but not the main objective.[4] The primary reason to stay in business, start a new business, or volunteer full time is to maintain a daily regimen of productive activity. Working out at the regular gym is nice, but it's not enough. You must also work out at the self-esteem gym by making important contributions to the world around you.

Case Study

I pursued a well-known author and speaker to appear at one of my conferences for his full fee. He, like I, was 64 at the time. He told me he was retired and not making any appearances. My wife and I had dinner with him and his wife, and I was able to cajole him to appear. But he told me he'd be there only for his 90 minutes, and I should have a car with the motor running and door open ready to whisk him away at the 91st minute.

At dinner with the group the evening before, I found him a *bon vivant*, actively engaged with everyone, telling stories, the last to leave the table. The next morning, he arrived at 8:00 p.m. for coffee with the group and proceeded to get everyone in an informal circle and address them about his work and beliefs. I had to call a halt at 9:00 p.m. and begin his formal session. At 10:30 p.m., with his car waiting outside and his time expired, he asked me if he could take another 10 minutes. He took 30 before I had to ask him to stop to remain on our schedule.

Retired? He hated retirement. This was his *milieu*. I asked his wife what on Earth he would do to keep himself busy. "Oh," she said happily, "we have a lot of friends and many interests."

I'd wager not enough of either. He was getting old beyond his time because he was artificially and arbitrarily removed from what he loved doing and the sizable contribution he could continue to make to others.

The "State of Confidence" Has All the Electoral Votes

Think of people who have immediately impressed you, whether at work, social gatherings, civic meetings, recreational events, or another venue. Write four *common characteristics* that made them impressive here:

1. _____
2. _____
3. _____
4. _____

Now go back and circle the characteristics that you think you possess and express on a regular basis.

How did you do?

Here's my point, relating to the condition I've been calling "confidence": There are really just a few characteristics and behaviors that demonstrate confidence to others and, commensurately, just a few tactics you need to maintain it. This expression of confidence (expertise, authority, wisdom, direction, intelligence, purpose) defies age and circumstance. That's why it's a critical condition for continued influence, power, and control as we mature.

I imagine that most readers listed personal assets like these:

- Assertiveness
- Persuasion
- Language
- Calmness
- Storytelling
- Experience
- Expertise
- Humor

And I'd guess that many readers feel that they possess two or three of the traits they listed in impressive people. I'd like to provide a slightly different view, and I'll start with a story of my own.

A couple of years ago, political strategist James Carville was a guest at one of my events. We were talking at one point over some Maker's Mark (his favorite bourbon) when I asked him why he thought Bill Clinton was so charismatic. I had never met Clinton, but everyone I knew who had met him, no matter their politics, mentioned his charisma.

Carville explained that when Clinton entered a room, he immediately sought the person who was least comfortable, the lowest ranking, the most intimidated, and went to that person to chat. He put him or her at ease, let everyone else wait, and showed genuine interest in the individual he was speaking with. "That trait," said Carville sipping his drink, "made him eminently likeable and impressive."

I'm going to suggest to you some perhaps unlikely elements for not merely possessing but expressing confidence:

1. Demonstrate interest in others. People who are insecure usually talk far too much about themselves, trying to build their credentials and repute all the time. People who are confident don't feel the need to do so and thus have plenty of time to learn what other people do. I once flew to Australia for 13 hours sitting next to Dolly Parton. She spent 95 percent of the time we chatted asking about my work. I later asked her road manager, who was sitting behind us, if she was always like that. "Absolutely," he said, "I've never met anyone who wasn't charmed by Dolly Parton."

2. Speak with volume. Projecting your voice in all situations demonstrates poise and belief. When I coached Miss America and Miss USA candidates in interviewing, I had them answer my questions from two rooms away. I'm not suggesting that volume beats accuracy, but I am telling you that volume builds trust and belief.[5] Find me an impressive person who mumbles. I have never seen one.

3. Use metaphors, examples, and stories. I referred to this idea in Chapter 3. Your language has to be colorful and illustrative. One of my favorite theater reviews is from John Mason Brown of a production of *King Lear*: "He played the king as if afraid someone else would play the ace."[6] Antoine de Riverol once said of a two-line poem, "Very nice, but there are dull stretches." I once sat at a business meeting where a vice president said a new idea he suggested was "global in impact," when the CEO said with a smile, "I think it's even bigger than that!" You need to learn to think and speak that way.

4. You need to be phlegmatic. (Let's see if you remember that word from our earlier test.) You can't be easily ruffled or made uncomfortable. You have to be in the moment and respond to events and discourse you hadn't anticipated. People respect those who are calm under fire, not easily thrown, in control. These are behavioral attributes. No matter how expert at navigation or landings, an airline pilot will not be successful if, when a red light illuminates in the cockpit, he runs down the aisle shouting, "We're doomed!"

We've recently seen a US election in which the winner did not win the popular vote but did win the electoral vote, hence the title of this segment. You don't necessarily want to be popular; you want to be *respected* (Figure 4.1).

As we mature, we should seek trusted advisor status, both formally (in business) and informally (socially). That means that people may like us to varying degrees, but they truly respect us for the very elements mentioned above.

Where affection is high but respect is low, we may be a buddy but not someone to necessarily depend on for serious matters. Where respect is high but affection is low, we may be seen as an aloof expert. And where neither is high, we're merely a vendor in business and invisible socially.

When we have both, we are the vaunted "trusted advisor."

One of our great gifts and tools of leverage in our maturity is our ability to display confidence and therefore be trusted and, perhaps, even charismatic. Unlike a façade in Disneyland, however, what people see has to be real and have depth.

Becoming Consistent Amid Inconsistency

Peter Drucker once wrote about an "age of discontinuity."[7] He meant, a quarter century ago, that we were no longer living in sequential, predictable, orderly times. Today, we talk about industry and market disrupters (like Uber), but the phenomenon is exactly the same. We haven't been living in the world of the traditional corporate ladder, family dinner table, and stable economics for quite some time.

Yet some of us act as if we are.

The wisdom of experience is hard to compete with. You may be embarrassed that you once used a rotary phone or opened your garage door manually, but having lived through, say, the Cuban Missile Crisis gives you the perspective to deal much more calmly with ISIS today. No one today, despite the terrorist tactics, thinks the world might blow up, but many did in 1962, and with good reason. Remembering major league baseball pitchers who

Figure 4.1 *Respect and affection.*

threw complete games rather than the six innings they're hoped to last these days is a revealing experience. And most of all, having lived through and managed companies and people during hard times, it's far easier to do so again.

All of those experiences provide an automatic advantage to people with *true* experience (not the same experience 10 years in a row). However, if we get mired in the past, then we're expecting continuity in the face of massive discontinuity.

So, what's the trick of being consistent among inconsistencies?

The answer is to separate *process* from *content.*

Content is what you're working with, be it insurance, transportation, engineering, finance, entertainment, hospitality, law, and so forth. These elements change frequently. New laws are passed, old ones overturned, new aspects of law emerge (ownership of frozen human eggs or underwater minerals). New financial investments emerge and old ones are abandoned. Entertainment becomes largely home centered, while engineering is based on three-dimensional duplications.

Process is about *how* you deal with your content, and it is relatively stable. For example:

- To solve a problem, you must remove its cause (an oil leak caused by a poor seal). To simply live with the effects of the problem, you use adaptive action (you put an extra quart of oil in the car every month, which we had to do with every Jaguar we ever owned).
- To make a decision, you need to know your destination (objective), various ways to reach it (alternatives), and attendant risks along the way that require mitigation (adverse consequences).
- In planning, you need to avoid problems (preventive actions such as separating combustible materials), deal with problems that may occur anyway (sprinkler systems and insurance as contingent actions), and put proper triggers in place (fire alarms).
- In conflict resolution, you need to find out if the disagreement is over the destination (in which case there must be an "owner" of the issue,

who decides) or over the routes (in which case, you need to create compromise among participants or create a new option that everyone can live with).

- In negotiation, you identify your "musts" (items that are critical to your success and cannot be bartered away) versus your "wants" (which are merely desirable and can be used as bargaining chips).
- In evaluating others' performance, you need metrics indicating whether they've met the expectations, failed to meet them, or exceeded them, and their buy-in on the measures.

You get the idea? The processes of excellent decision-making or nego-tiation—or twenty other important processes—haven't changed for eons.[8] Cavemen took routes designed to avoid the most vicious predators, and the Wright brothers sought out the causes of their early failures before they merely patched up the plane or built a new one.

Thus, your power is to adjust to the inconsistencies of the content around us by mastering the consistencies of excellent judgment, processes, and applications of talents. These processes can be learned at any time and mastered in short order. For many years, I've had senior business leaders, nonprofit executives, and successful entrepreneurs tell me that they simply acted "naturally" and had no set methodology responsible for their success.

They were either unaware of their own methods or were lying!

What I found when I deconstructed their styles is that they had expert processes that they either never bothered to articulate or didn't choose to (for fear of others using their own devices against them in a competitive world). I asked a famous psychologist once how he could so readily look at psychometric test results and immediately reach conclusions about some-one's behavioral predispositions, never having met or observed the person.

"I simply look at the *gestalt* of the results," he said dismissively, as though addressing a graduate class.

"Tell me what you do first, second, and third," I demanded.

Once he did that, I knew his process. He first checked to see if there were sufficient responses for a valid interpretation, he then checked for internal contradictions, and so forth. I was actually using a process to determine his processes!

Becoming consistent in your use of processes will enable you to deal with any content. You can never be "passed by" or "outmoded" or "not up to date" with constantly changing content, because the way you handle it is what really matters. It's why I could consult with oil, media, insurance, manufacturing, transportation, and pharmaceutical industries with ease. They have content experts falling out of the rafters, and those experts are periodically replaced by new content experts when disruptions occur (e.g., in moving from chemical film processing to electronic photography you no longer need bench chemists, you need experts in digital media).

People who are seen as old-fashioned are wedded to obsolete content. They insist on security guards instead of security cameras. Yet the *process* of providing security remains the same: employ multiple levels of redundancy, 24-hour monitoring, and so on.

Your assets of maturity, wisdom, and experience are magnified by your ability to master the processes that apply no matter what content you find yourself dealing with, no matter the type of discontinuity, no matter how abrupt the change. Automobiles, airlines, trains, and ships may be beneficiaries of the computer age, but their scheduling and speed and safety nonetheless present continuing process issues.

It doesn't matter how fast things are moving, therefore; what matters is how fast you can apply the correct processes to others' well-being and effectiveness.

Achieving Self-Validation

As we age, we should realize that we're "valid" (the quality of being sound)! After all, we have a wake behind our boat of years of accomplishment, success, and effectiveness. Yet...

We discussed self-esteem earlier in this chapter, and the need for that muscle to be worked out daily. Validation, as we tend to apply it to a position or argument, means "authentic" or "logical" or even "legally binding." As we apply it to ourselves, however, we tend to mean "having the right to be here," "belonging," "justified."

There are two sources for validation: internal and external. For the former, we are able to declare ourselves legitimate and contributing. That is a healthy position. For the latter, we need another person or group or body to do that for us. That is a dangerous position.

Have you seen these people with 14 initials after their names? The string of credentials is sort of like a serpent that keeps chasing the person's proper name.[9] These are desperate attempts to demonstrate external validation—various groups and bodies touch a sword to your shoulders and pronounce you a knight in their kingdom. People who come to me asking about the various "coaching universities" and the bewildering certificates (and initials) they bestow always prompt this question: Who certifies the certifiers? (Said more eloquently by Juvenal, "*Sed quis custodiet ipsos custodes?*"—Who shall guard us from the guardians?)

When I pointed out this silliness on social media platforms, scores of people, all hemorrhaging initials, unfriended, unlinked, unfollowed, and unfrocked me. They went ballistic over my implication that their need for meaningless external validation was a fool's errand. As a matter of fact, I don't even believe that MD is important after a doctor's name if that doctor is writing a letter to the editor about a nonmedical subject.

But what does all this have to do with you and me daily?

My son called home from the University of Miami and asked to speak to me, not his mother. All of you who have children know that this request is *never* an indication of good news.

He told me that, after 4 years in the drama department, he was to appear in the final performance, *The Grapes of Wrath.* He had anticipated playing the lead, Tom Joad, but the department had opted to bring in an outsider, a graduate student, to play the part and offered my son another role in the production.

"How do you feel?" I asked.

"I feel hurt, angry, betrayed, disappointed, frustrated, and confused," he blurted out.

"And why are you calling me?" I asked.

"I want to know how I should feel."

"You should feel exactly the way you do. I would."

"You would?" (There was an exhalation of breath here.)

"Of course, but the question is, once you get through those feelings, *what will you do about them?* We both know you can boycott the play, demand another audition, appeal to the department head, or take the role offered and do a great job. It's not what happens to you, Jason, it's what you do about it."

I had validated Jason's feelings, because whatever our feelings are, they are valid. Then he was able to make an intelligent decision to take the other role, in which he was excellent. He admitted later that the guy they brought in was much better in the lead than he would have been. That was a huge growth experience, far beyond landing a starring role in a college performance.

That's an expected, reasonable reaction for a child and a student, but it's not good for an adult and a parent, or for a business person or board member, or for a community activist. We have to understand and appreciate that our feelings are valid *and we are valid,* and what matters are our actions and behaviors.

In the world of professional speaking (the source of some of those initials that cling like gum on your shoe), there are many fine speakers who are client-oriented and focused on meeting the client's needs in their speech. There are others who are audience-centered and seek to create an entertaining time for the group. But then there are some who are speaker-centered and are seeking validity. These are the people who crave the standing ovations, who want perfect 10s across the board on their "smile sheets" (evaluation sheets), and who want to be validated by the audience.

That means of course, that one demurral, one poor score, can be devastating. One speaker at one of my events went up on her lines (omitting about 15 minutes of a memorized speech) and therefore finished early. She seemed flustered (and was too shaken to simply ask for questions to fill the time), but I thanked her and she received nice applause.

Later, she asked what my impression was. I told her she was fine. She broke down in tears. (I seem to have that effect on women.) She told me that "fine" wasn't good enough, she had to be "great."

That's quite a burden, one that I can happily live without.

We seek validation too often from others instead of simply reassuring ourselves. Think about it. Here are some of the habits of those who constantly attempt to get external validation.

- We regularly ask others if we've made the right decision.
- Even after a win or a victory, we ask if we could have done it still better.
- We want someone's buy-in before we act, even though the decision is ours.
- We practice consensus management and decision-making, thereby avoiding accountability for the tough calls required of our own jobs.
- We place more emphasis on what people think of us than what we actually accomplish.
- We lose perspective, looking for quantity approval, not quality approval.

In the film *Mr. Saturday Night*, Billy Crystal wows an audience at a mountain resort. They're screaming and yelling as the comic leaves the stage. His manager, in the wings, says, "Kid, name your price, you're a hit!" But Crystal is unhappy.

"What's the problem?" says the manager, "They loved you."

"Did you see the guy at table five?" asks Crystal. "He didn't laugh once all night."

Comics are notoriously insecure. There's no need for you to be. Stop seeking approval from others. As we mature, we should be granting approval.

Especially to ourselves.

Notables

Johann Wolfgang von Goethe, 83. Finished writing *Faust* after working on it for 60 years.

Mary Delany, 72. Invented paper collage.

Laura Ingalls Wilder, 65. Began writing series that included *Little House on the Prairie*.

Fauja Singh, 89. Ran his first marathon (and still runs in them).

Clara Peller, 81. Became the "Where's the beef?" woman for Wendy's.

Grandma Moses, 78. Achieved fame as an artist.

Harry Bernstein, 96. Wrote the highly successful *The Invisible Wall: A Love Story That Broke Barriers*.

Colonel Harland Sanders, 65. Founded Kentucky Fried Chicken (KFC).

Notes

1. Bureau of Labor Statistics, reported in "More workers are staying on the job past 65," *Boston Globe*, June 12, 2017.
2. Ibid.
3. For example: Comfort Keepers, "Senior Mind," http://www.comfortkeepers.com/home/care-services/senior-caregiving/senior-mind.
4. However, being paid is an excellent metric to judge the degree to which you are valued and are being successful, whether someone else is paying you or you're paying yourself.
5. Unbelievably, when people ask me how I can publish so many books—more than 60—I tell them I pursue volume over accuracy. At least half say, "Oh, I see," and walk away!
6. "John Mason Brown quotes," Brainyquote.com, https://www.brainyquote.com/quotes/quotes/j/johnmasonb142456.html.
7. Peter Drucker, *The Age of Discontinuity*, Routledge, New York, 1992.
8. For example, see my book, *Process Consulting*, Jossey-Bass/Pfeiffer, San Francisco, 2002.
9. To show you how silly this is, I have been bestowed with PhD, CMC, FCMC, CSP, and CPAE by various august bodies. That's 17 letters that, if accompanied by $2, will get me on a bus.

CHAPTER 5

Critical Thinking Is Redundant

Every old dog I've ever had learned new tricks if the tricks were in its self-interest. ALL thinking should be critical thinking, and we should streamline it so we escape old norms (blaming people long since removed from our lives). There are excellent techniques to remain forceful and innovative in one's thinking and implementation. As we grow older, we need to move from dealing with change to creating it.

Occam's Razor and the Beauty of Directness

William of Ockham lived his adult years at the beginning of the 14th century. He was a Franciscan friar and theologian who postulated that, among competing hypotheses, the one with the fewest assumptions should be selected. Over the years, it's been interpreted to mean that the simplest explanation is probably the correct explanation, all other things being equal.

Although that is not universally true in complex decisions, it is remarkably accurate in daily life. There is an old consulting rubric that goes like this:

Client: It hurts when I do this.
Consultant: Stop doing that.
Client: It stopped hurting!
Consultant: That will be $50,000.

We tend to believe that complicating things—adding complexity— makes the solutions and decision more elegant. But that's untrue, it simply makes them more difficult to implement.

The late Russ Ackoff, a brilliant consultant, was once asked by London's transit authority to devise a way to stop buses from being delayed and piling up on each other while conductors laboriously collected money and dispensed tickets on two levels of the bus. Countless experts had suggested all manner of things, including increasing the number of conductors, changing schedules, and collecting when people disembarked.

Ackoff told them to take the conductors off the buses and put them on the street corners at the bus stops. It worked immediately.[1]

As we mature—as the horizon draws closer—we have less time to fritter away, less time for trial and error, less time to go around the block when our destination is simply next door. We don't need to be blunt, but we do need to be direct in our language and in our plans.

If we suspect something is wrong with family members, we should ask them about it.

If we find ourselves in need of help, we should request it.

If we are having difficulty with a relationship, we should confront it.

If we're unhappy with our life, we should change it.

Similarly, we need to find the express lanes and even shortcuts to destinations, assuming we're not just out for a leisurely drive. (We need to suggest taking the conductors off the buses and not conform to the traditional configurations.)

Ask yourself these questions in business and in life:

- What is the simplest, quickest, and easiest possible resolution?
- Can I use it without a downside or adverse consequences?
- If there are consequences, can I manage and/or ameliorate them?
- Is there anything important stopping me from moving forward with this plan?

We often don't move fast enough because we lean toward overprotection. At the outset of this book, I referred to generational attributes that we tend to assign. The current generation of young adults may be the most overprotected, coddled, and insulated in history, with "trigger warnings," "safe zones," and parents complaining about too much homework. For now, that's their problem, but don't allow it to become yours.

We don't need protection, we need action. We need to accept prudent risk (not gambles) and understand that *the search for perfection kills excellence*. Success trumps perfection, and no airplane ride, meal, hotel stay, or relationship you've ever experienced or ever will experience has been perfect. Perfection is not only unattainable, it's unnecessary for success and happiness.

Thus, develop the habit of moving imperfectly forward with the confidence and knowledge that we all make midcourse corrections every day. As you drive your car and listen to music or talk to a passenger, you are constantly making minute adjustments to the steering wheel. They're not extreme, but they are important to keep you on the road.

Life is the same way. Small, easy, quick adjustments help you stay on life's road.

Here are some of the easy, simple, quick routes you can often take.

- Argue about principle but not about taste. Your kids' education is one thing, but which restaurant you visit is quite another. The office décor isn't all that critical, but the customer service policy is.
- Use objective reasoning, observed behavior, and evidence. Telling someone that he's not a team player is nowhere near as useful as saying, "You're late for all of our meetings, which wastes everyone else's time." Telling your partner that she's disorganized is less helpful than saying, "When was the last time you remember using your keys?"
- Generalize positives and isolate negatives. If your child misses a kick in a game, tell her it was a tough kick, not that she's awkward or a lousy athlete. Don't tell a colleague he can't sell, just acknowledge that, on this particular day, he didn't make a sale to a certain prospect. Conversely, when your child makes a great kick, don't praise the kick, tell her that she's a terrific athlete (or with a high test score, an

outstanding scholar). When your colleague makes the sale, don't call it his lucky day but tell him he's a champion marketer.

- Stop second-guessing. Don't tell yourself that if it looks too good to be true, it can't be worthwhile. The shortest distance between two points is still a straight line. Make the process simple by asking these questions, variations of the ones above:
  - What are the risks in taking this action?
  - Am I able to prevent the risks and/or ameliorate their effects?
  - Is the reward worth the risk management?

  This way you stop worrying about unseen traps and deal with the real issues you can control.

- Recognize that you have more control than you think. You can't control the weather or the tax code. But you can control your own behaviors and strongly influence most environments. Always have a Plan B. (It's possible to move the birthday party from the backyard to the basement.) We spend far too much time trying to make an unsuccessful Plan A work, rather than just quickly going to our Plan B. Of course, that demands that you always have a Plan B and even a Plan C.

The ability to use our maturity, experience, education, and wisdom is a simple and quick advantage that gives us great power. This is an age of high tech, artificial intelligence, and drones, true; but it's also an age in which judgment is in critical demand (Volkswagen, Wells Fargo, Uber, and others are examples where judgment was ruinous).

Young people are understandably immersed in technology, but they can't be immersed in wisdom. That's the province of those of us who are threescore and more. But we have to manifest it. We have to assert it.

You might believe that extra time boarding a plane, senior discounts, seating concessions, government health coverage, social security payments, and so forth are amenities and benefits due to you. I don't. Surely, the incapacitated and disadvantaged should be taken care of. But that's true for people at *any* age. When society makes the assumption that merely living longer creates a disabled state, that simple longevity results in a weaker person; that is a belief so crass that I scarcely know where to begin with it.

If the easiest route is usually the best, then the best route here is to understand that we are all capable of huge contributions, that technology is all around us, but wisdom is rare.

Finding Causes, Not Blame

Every problem has a cause. That cause could be human error, equipment breakdown, malfunction, acts of God (don't scoff, the phrase is in insurance and other legal contracts), and so on. The dinosaurs, having existed for 129 million years or so, were wiped out by a meteorite hitting the Yucatan. Even if they were sentient beings, not much can be done about that.

Our problem today, exacerbated by the media, is that we constantly seek *culpability* instead of cause, *blame* instead of bare facts. It's more relieving to blame someone (instant gratification), it's often vainglorious (I told them so), and it's certainly less work (the process takes mere minutes).

Maturity and its power is in recognizing that we need to search for cause.

You can't remove a problem unless you know its cause. You can certainly ameliorate its symptoms, but you can't remove the problem itself by merely addressing its effects. You can place a bucket under a leak in the roof, but the leak will continue and you'll have to empty the bucket. The solution is to remove the cause by patching the roof (since you can't remove the rain). In a relationship, you're not going to be able to communicate with a resistant family member until you recognize and admit the cause of the poor feelings. There may be an old slight or a forgotten and unpaid debt. But dismissing the person or talking through an intermediary does not remove the root cause.

My colleague and coauthor on one book,[2] Phil Symchych, a financial expert, points out that most businesses cite poor sales or revenue or cash flow as a "problem." Those are not problems, they are symptoms of the problem, and the cause is poor marketing. Cutting costs does not improve marketing; therefore, cost cutting is merely a band aid that many organizations, large and small, believe is actually a solution. It's not.

It's the bucket under the leak.

Similarly, you can't prevent a future problem's *occurrence* without preventing its cause. If you want to prevent fire in a house you're building, extinguishers, sprinklers, escape routes, and insurance policies won't help you. They will only mitigate the effects of a fire, perhaps reducing damage and injury, but the fire will have occurred.

Preventive action is aimed at cause: ensuring that electrical and gas connections are consistent with code, using nonflammable materials, prohibiting smoking, installing lighting rods, and so forth. Note that you can't *guarantee* prevention; therefore, contingent actions like insurance should always be in place. But you can seriously reduce the risk of the problem by trying to eliminate the causes of that problem.

If you're going to a business meeting and you fear that people won't understand the technical aspects, it's probably not the best idea to send the details in advance, because participants will still be confused by them (perhaps more so without your explanations). A preventive action would more properly be using simple graphics on slides to show connections that are difficult to visualize when they are merely read.

Yet what we actually experience in many cases are questions and comments such as, "How can you expect salespeople to pay attention to significant technical issues?" or "If Ralph is in the meeting, he's going to ask stupid questions," or "What can you expect from someone her age?"

I think you can see I'm not exaggerating. We surrender power when we join the blame game, because we will ultimately be its victims at some point. We retain power when we rise above it and direct others to find cause or prevent cause instead of finding blame and shame.

People feel guilty because others heap guilt on them, or they wallow in their own guilt by bearing the blame for something. Yet, there's the great old story about a person who made a million-dollar error and asked the boss if a resignation were required. The answer: "I just invested a million bucks for you to learn something important, why would I fire you now?"

As I write this, I'm observing the worst polarization in the United States in my memory. Positions on abortion, gender identity, health care, immigration, climate, and other matters aren't simply being debated in public (as they should be) but rather are the levers of blame used by either side against the other. It's no longer a question of finding the cause of the problem—or even the cause of the disagreement—but rather of blaming anyone who doesn't agree with you.

If you don't believe in human contribution to profound climate change you're called a "denier." If you believe that it's a woman's decision to have control over her own biology, including abortion, you're called a "baby killer." The blame game has usurped the arguments, taken over the playing field, and killed rational discourse.

In the business world we've often created silos and turf that are owned by one area, and a warning to "keep off the grass" is the normal state of affairs. Internecine warfare saps energy and diverts talent.

As you can see in Figure 5.1, organizations (and people) have 100 percent of energy and talent to disseminate. (I've never understood what it means to "give 110 percent." It's an empty admonition.) So the critical issue becomes: To what end are your energy and talent directed? Ideally, and in the best organizations I've seen, it's 90 percent to the customer, product,

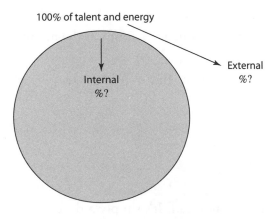

Figure 5.1 *Internal and external focus.*

service, or relationship (external), and 10 percent internal; it's hard to completely eradicate office gossip and intrigue.

However, I worked in a consulting firm in Princeton at one point in my career where the split was 90 percent internal and 10 percent external. We all vied for certain perquisites and bonuses, offices and favors, so the clients received little attention unless they screamed. I'm sure you've observed the same.

It's vital that we focus on finding cause before we take permanent actions. We can take temporary, adaptive actions, like that bucket under the leak or borrowing money to pay bills, until we improve the marketing. But only a focus on cause will truly correct and/or prevent serious problems. No matter how fabulous and effective the sprinkler system, the fire will have already occurred, with attendant financial loss, injury, time loss, and embarrassment.

If you want to stop being blamed, simply respond, "Why don't we find the cause of the problem, rather than a scapegoat?" To avoid the blame game in the future, ask, "Have we considered every possible option to prevent the causes of this potential problem?" You want to be the one who sets the stage for examining cause and not culpability.

Sometimes humans are clearly the cause. Someone was asleep, distracted, poorly trained, incompetent. If you focus on the cause, then you can prevent its recurrence or duplication in others. I don't think TSA security people allow weapons through checkpoints because they are inept or don't care. I think they are bored and it's hard to maintain vigilance in highly repetitive situations. Consequently, firing the agent who missed the test gun or bomb isn't the answer, but more frequent rotations at the monitoring station probably is.

That seems simple enough. But only the wise person suggests it and is willing to implement it.

Exploiting Change

Change is neither good nor bad. It's simply a difference between what was and what now is, or what is to be. I don't mean to be Zen about that, but all change is time related. Any distinction between today and yesterday or today and tomorrow takes place over time.

No one is afraid of or naturally resistant to change. I know that flies in the face of conventional wisdom, but conventional wisdom is neither conventional nor wise. (Otherwise, it's great.) We are often burdened with the horrible admonition "You can't teach an old dog new tricks." That is empirically false. (My dogs, at ages 13 and 14, constantly learned new ways to steal food and to escape the yard and run around the neighborhood. They actually became more adept and more confident as they aged. They became wise.)

It's also a horrible example of bigotry presented in a deceiving message. Suggested as a truism, not to be challenged, it's actually a bias against anyone over the arbitrary age the utterer identifies as the threshold of incompetence. Actually, not unlike my dogs, we all gain confidence, experience, and ingenuity at creating and exploiting change as we age.

We all change our plans, short term and long term, constantly. We adjust a vacation given weather or transportation problems. We modify our approach to customers and clients given competitive actions. We change our investment strategies given new market conditions. We change our marital status, doctors, place of residence, religious affiliation, and even food intake based on a wide variety of actual, anticipated, or even simply perceived changes.

So let's dispatch the notion that we are sedentary beings who eschew change as a default mechanism, and that change is somehow avoidable. Here's a different kind of truth.

We thrive on change because it increases our chances of improving the status quo. It shakes things up in ways that the normal state of affairs can't. It creates variety and excitement in our lives. It demonstrates our resilience and grit. I make the case that we *require* change in our lives in order to be fulfilled, challenged, involved, and embraced.

Thus, change can be negative (I began smoking) or positive (I've given up smoking). The key here is *intentionality*. Are we capable and equipped to create and make the most of (exploit) change? *That is not an age issue, that is an intrinsic motivational issue.*

First, we're not an "old dog," even though those dogs do just fine. And second, we can learn any trick we so choose. But they must be reasonable. Even a young dog can't learn to fly.

The second issue with change, beyond the fact that we all engage in it more eagerly and constantly than the bromides would suggest, is that the *result* of change isn't threatening, but the *journey* often is. You can see the ambiguous aspect of the journey in Figure 5.2.

The desired result of the change—weight loss, promotion, divorce, tour of India, education—is usually just dandy. Countless executives have rallied the troops with glorified visions of their new jobs, generals have spoken eloquently of the fruits of victory, Romeo swept Juliet off her feet (as did Tony with Maria in the modern version, *West Side Story*), and the thought of heaven has certainly been more attractive to believers than that of hell.

But getting to that future state can be a real problem! People despise dating; in college, they labor under tough coursework and the accumulation of debt; they're not crazy about charging the enemy over open ground; they worry about their job security in a new, automated operation. Great leaders get on a horse and say, "Follow me, I know the way." Not-so-great ones push their people out there first.[3]

If you want to exert influence on old, young, and peers alike, explain the journey. Light some lights. Show the way.

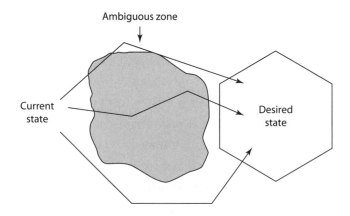

Figure 5.2   *The ambiguous zone.*

Many managers reached key positions without ever encountering hard times. It's relatively easy to manage in good times, but in so doing we learn nothing of managing in adversity. Who does? Those of us with the maturity and experience to have endured both. We can show the way, light the light.

To increase your influence and control, you must be the confident one during the journey, exploring new ways through the new territory, not hiding under a desk with those who want others to take the first steps. You can't be a pack animal, you have to be a maverick.[4] And because so many people are shirking and awaiting the leader, it's easy to get on the horse, especially since no one is shooting at you here!

How do you most readily exploit change? Here are my suggestions:

- Don't be the devil's advocate. Find ways to support change, not reflexively resist it. Focus on making the journey not just tolerable but attractive.
- Be enthusiastic. Enthusiasm is contagious. No one builds statues to critics, they build them for creators.
- Volunteer in a key role. Walk your talk. Take responsibility for the initiative, innovation, or project.
- Create safety for people. Think about our earlier discussion about finding likely causes of future problems so that they can be prevented and eliminated (and/or deleterious effects ameliorated).
- Present the adversity of the alternative. That is, no action is often worse than imperfect action. The competition advances, the bleeding continues, the opportunity is lost. (If you think education is expensive, try ignorance.)
- Use your experiences to demonstrate that much tougher journeys have been successfully undertaken, and explain why. Provide guidance from someone who has "been there and done that" (and has the tee-shirt to prove it).
- Rally people past temporary setbacks. No journey is without error, detour, and disappointment, but those are virtually never fatal. Get back on your horse.

- Learn from the experience. You're not an "old dog" simply providing guidance. What can you learn to use again and build on in the future? This is a process, not an event.

Change is inevitable and we're better at handling it than we think. But only the gifted few—the mature and wise—can exploit change better than anyone else.

Methodical Innovation

There is a synergy about critical thinking, personal and professional success, and innovation that's important to appreciate and practice. In fact, there are few devices as effective in overcoming bias about competencies and stereotypes about inclusion as the methodical application of innovation.

"Methodical innovation" may sound oxymoronic. But that's because people associate innovation with a visit from the muse, the lightning strike of a new idea, a lucky discovery. But, in fact, if that were the case, we would have a hell of a lot fewer innovations.

Innovation involves perspiration. There is a methodology, a process, and it's the worst kind of hard work: mental hard work.

Here's the basic process of new ideas, in my experience:

1. **Accident.** Someone discovers through happenstance that something will unexpectedly work: Arm & Hammer Baking Soda, accidentally left open in a refrigerator, proved to be an ideal deodorizer. A poorly working adhesive formula was superb as the temporary adhesion needed for Post-it® Notes.
2. **Reaction.** Someone wanted to signal a change of lanes in his car without having to use conventional turn signals, which were often left on for miles and miles. So a short, three-burst signal that turns

itself off was created, and some cars now have a warning buzzer that sounds when the directional signal is left on for more than a minute.

3. **Opportunism.** You see an opportunity to create something that customers didn't realize they need. When banks and department stores and insurance companies were sending massive amounts of bills by regular mail, some firms realized that this was basically a method of distribution and could be highly valuable if advertisements and promotions were included in the mailings. It costs money to send bills unless someone is paying you to put something in that same envelope.

Case Study

An accountant in Rhode Island named Bill Janikies had a fast food restaurant called Burger King as a client. When he realized how much money the franchise was capable of generating, he cashed in his practice and bought one. When he passed away at 84, his company owned more than 100 restaurants and country clubs. He saw an opportunity and never looked back.

4. **Conformist innovation.** This occurs when someone decides to make a vast improvement on an already-existing process, product, service, or entity. Uber, I believe, is in this category because it essentially took an already-existing industry, taxi transportation, and vastly improved it with clean cars, choice of vehicles, trained drivers, GPS summoning, central billing, and so on. Lyft has simply copied Uber (as have cab companies, which now have their own apps).

5. **Nonconformist innovation.** This occurs with totally new ideas rather than mere improvements on existing ones. Powered flight was an example, as were submarines. But I would also put binge-watching in this category (shows produced in total and all episodes released at once), and I would place Amazon.com and tele-health in this category as well.

Case Study

Being a copycat doesn't work, not so much because you are always second or worse, but because *you don't understand the original innovation rationale.*

When Mercedes-Benz was a client and Lexus was trying to compete on the basis of safety and engineering, Mercedes engineers took me to an area where they dismantled Lexus automobiles; reverse engineering is very common in the industry. They showed me a roof feature on the Mercedes that carried water off the roof, away from the windows, and down to the street.

On the Lexus, the same feature looked to be present, but it wasn't functional, only cosmetic, and didn't carry the water away. Lexus had copied the style but failed to implement its purpose.

We need to separate innovation from problem-solving. In problem-solving, the emphasis is to restore performance to previous levels, while in innovation, the emphasis is on creating *entirely new levels.* As you can see in Figure 5.3, we are now engaged in raising the bar to new heights, not trying to find the cause of a problem so that we can merely restore the bar to its former height.

Joseph Schumpeter is usually credited with defining innovation (and capitalism) as "creative destruction."[5]

The importance to us here is that our economy advances through innovation and, especially, nonconformist innovation. Therefore, the more you can provide new ideas and insights of this nature, the more valuable, essential, and regarded you become; the more control you possess; and the more your maturity is seen as an asset.

Thus, master the *process* of methodical innovation:

1. Search for new, nonconformist ideas.
2. Perform a risk/reward assessment of their value. All innovation involves some risk; the issue is the degree of the payoff versus the costs of controlling the risks.

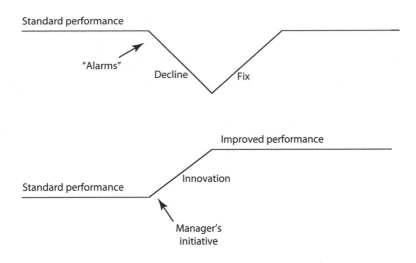

Figure 5.3 *Problem-solving and innovation.*

3. Create support and synergies among all key parties.
4. Create an implementation plan. Note that, in this case, we want to find the causes of the new standards and promote them, not prevent them! (If a cause of greater good health is the cessation of smoking, then let's promote a strong factor, such as healthier families through the absence of second-hand smoke or the ability to play with one's grandchildren, in our educational campaigns.)[6]

Case Study

In the 1980s, someone in the bowels of American Airlines's marketing department—not the executive suite—came up with the idea of free points for every mile traveled, resulting in free tickets—the Advantage Program. Today, a global industry is based on airline, hotel, and credit card use, restaurant visits, and so on. That was nonconformist innovation started at a low level with a good idea and a responsive management.

In your work, your family, your social involvements, your civic duties, and your interests, become focused on innovation to improve people's lives, business results, and health. When you do this, you become irreplaceable, not because of your tool kit or physical activity but because of your expertise and insights.

So stop trying to solve problems unless they're critical, and start trying to create new ways to do things that will be critical. That's how you remain vibrant and important without a time limit.

Notables

Wally Blume, 62. Started a dairy business that became Denali Flavors, which now has more than $85 million in sales.

Lisa Gable, 70. Invented a new kind of bra strap; was still running the company at 85 (Strap-Mate).

Jeanne Dowell, 80. Began Green Buddha Clothing; provides a percentage of all profits to charity.

Edmond Hoyle, 70. Began to establish the rules of card games.

Cornelius Vanderbilt, 70. Began buying railroads.

Katsusuke Yanagisawa, 71. Climbed Mount Everest (oldest ever).

Barbara Hillary, 75. Cancer survivor; became first black woman to reach the North Pole.

Benjamin Spock, 83. Famed baby doctor began his work for world peace.

Marc Chagall, 90. First living artist to be exhibited at the Louvre.

Notes

1. Russell Ackoff, *The Art of Problem Solving*, Wiley, New York, 1987.
2. Phil Symchych and Alan Weiss, *The Business Wealth Builders*, Business Expert Press, New York, 2015.

3. The highest percentage loss of officer grades during the Civil War—our bloodiest in history—was among brigadier generals, who led their brigades from the front, on a horse, highly visible to enemy sharpshooters. But, in so doing, the troops energetically followed. Today, the highest-ranking firefighting officer is usually the first one in the burning building. Generals, however, are in the rear.

4. See my book for more discussion on this phenomenon: *Million Dollar Maverick*, Bibliomotion, New York, 2016.

5. Wikipedia, "Creative Destruction," https://en.wikipedia.org/wiki/Creative_destruction.

6. And that's exactly why education, and not greater taxation and prices, has drastically reduced tobacco use in the United States.

CHAPTER 6

The Nongovernment Safety Net

We shut ourselves up in gated communities and condos where we only look at each other. After having children, we act as if we never want children living near us again. We become nondiverse and herd-like. But there are simple techniques to ensure that new energy keeps entering one's "system" and that we can be self-supporting and inter-act with a diverse community of our own making—virtually and in reality.

The Colleagues to Acquire and Sustain

We've been fascinated by "safety nets" over the years. I began this book with a description of the math used 75 years ago to create the social security system. It's now flawed and outdated. Yet even at the time it was developed, social security was not meant as "lifestyle perpetuation" but rather as a backstop, an augmentation to personal savings, business retirement accounts, and the support of extended family.

The same applies to the minimum wage. We seem to view it today in horror as being incapable of supporting even rudimentary needs of a family. Yet, that was not its intent. The purpose was to provide a minimum wage in part-time work, transitory work, and second jobs. It was never intended to represent the pay needed to support a family as a sole source. But that's what it's been interpreted as (and universally, as more than 90 countries have such laws).

We have to begin thinking in terms of a personal security plan. Not a safety net, which implies that we've fallen and are trying not to hurt ourselves more seriously (many acrobats have been seriously injured falling into a safety net, an analogy I find quite apt) but a plan for assertive and personal control of our lives. Obviously, that control has to be based on today's actuarial tables and probabilities. (If you're 65, at this writing you can expect to live another 20 years, on average; if you're 75, you can expect to live another 11 years.)[1]

That support system is not merely, or even primarily, financial. There are more important elements, at work and at home, that will sustain you and contribute to your financial security. I'm going to leave the discussion of investments and assets and estate planning to the proper experts. There are a great many of them. But there aren't many people suggesting these other dimensions to examine for your personal security in perpetuity.

Here is a basic philosophy that will prevent you from becoming dependent, assuming you're no longer on top of your game, surrendering control: No one has the right to wealth without creating it, and no one has the right to happiness without creating it. The more assertive we are, the more successful we'll be. The more dependent we allow ourselves to become, the less successful we'll be.

Here are the dynamics of our approach to our own security:

1. Family. There is a tendency to attenuate family ties in these times. Some of it is the result of easier movement. Children go away to college, land jobs in different places, and marry or live with people whom they join in other countries. We also tend to label family members and tolerate them according to the labels. Aunt Joan is always good for sharing secrets and getting advice, but Uncle Henry drinks too much, and twice a year is the limit for his company.

But as we mature, family is important for support, intimacy, and perspective. People may indeed move more easily today, but we have the technology to get together more readily through email, Skype, Zoom, cell phones, and, perhaps by the time you read this, holographic images.[2] From our forties on, we should be maintaining, sustaining, and repairing (where necessary) family bonds.[3]

We don't need these family members so much for financial reasons, though help with the repayment of educational loans, uncovered medical costs, and natural disasters can make them critical. They are for *power*, the unfailing support of people who will be candid, let you know the fights to fight and the fights to skip, and be there for you—and you for them—when adversity strikes or good fortune erupts. I think the greatest single work of American literature is about the Joad family and their travails in one of the worst times in our history.[4]

2. Friends. The notion of friends for life is nice but hardly mandatory. Many of us have them, many of us don't. Friends can be

- **Lifelong.** We retain the ties from childhood, whether close by or at a distance.
- **Transitory.** Friends come and go in our lives based on work, education, geography, hobbies, civic involvement, memberships, and so forth. Some of these friendships become lifelong, but most fade once we leave the common environment.
- **Leveraged.** We develop friendships with those who can help us and whom we can help. These relationships are almost always reciprocal if they are to work well. I may help you with your business venture while you help me with my golf game. You help me gain membership into private clubs, while I share with you my wine expertise.
- **Virtual.** These are largely dependent on social media and other platforms where we form often quite tenuous connections. These are friends in the sense that we have continual communication and interaction, but most of the contact occurs in a public and/or group setting. Nonetheless, such friendships often usually form around common interests, and the bonds can be quite genuine.

3. Connections. These are the relationships we build with others who are neither family nor friends but are highly valuable. The connection may be a politician for whom we vote and to whose campaign we contribute, who in turn can help us through a bureaucratic tangle or arrange a tour of the White House. It may be a member of the clergy who, in total secrecy, can help us with an important personal or family matter with objective and wise counsel.

These relationships and connections can be with people ranging from medical experts to ticket brokers, from financial professionals to handymen. But all are people who provide a distinctive kind of help—physical, mental, emotional, or spiritual—when it is needed. Life is too short to spend long periods of it standing in lines. We all need people—and need to retain the connections with people—who can metaphorically "cut the line."

I've never believed that a Harvard education is all that much better than one from Ohio State or UCLA or Rutgers (especially since the best faculty seldom deign to appear in the classroom), but I have realized that the *contacts* one makes at Harvard are probably superior to most. Life is about connections.

We can't afford to sacrifice or sever those connections as we mature. *In fact, we need them more than ever, and we need more of them than ever.* Hence, we need to prize, sustain, and build our connections continually in order to leverage our power and control.

This combination of family, friends, and connections is the true support system, far superior to any financial safety net provided by the government.

Personal Support Systems for the Ages

Our personal support is too important to be left to the government, employers, family, colleagues, or other people and institutions. These sources can be important but, ultimately, we are responsible for ourselves.

It's the abdication of this responsibility that causes genuine problems as we age. We become subliminally helpless. We come to expect the special seating, the handouts, the discounts, the exceptions. It occurs to me that it's like affirmative action for the aged. *Except affirmative action goals are to educate and employ people, not shuffle them off to the side.*

Let me be absolutely clear about this, and you may not appreciate my position at first, but hear me out: *Any exception made for people where they do not have to perform as others, behave as others, accept the accountabilities that others accept, or meet the standards that others must meet means, by definition, that those people are inferior.* That's right, the implicit belief that underlies all such favors, shortcuts, easements, and other special provisions is not one of courtesy or thoughtfulness, though that may be claimed and is the superficial reason.

The belief is that you and I can't perform the way others can, so we need an exception. And people who are granted exceptions have some weakness, liability, or inferiority. (And while those with physical disabilities, for example, may legitimately need additional supports, it is not the case merely because a person has attained some arbitrary age.)

A very young woman, in a fit of road rage, once stormed after me, screaming that I had cut her off. The epithet she kept using was "old man" (I was 58 at the time). I said to her, "Really? Is that the best you can do? Is that your best shot?" She was driving an old Volvo and I was driving a new Bentley. She couldn't use the language well and was overreacting to an imagined slight. Yet it was my age that she found most vulnerable, the target that she thought would hurt the most.

And therein I learned an important lesson: We all feel younger than our chronological ages, barring serious illness.[5] But others, who possess certain biases, don't see us that way. They see age, most of the time, as a drawback.

"Most of the time," not "all of the time." Why not? Because when we exhibit power, control, and expertise *age becomes an asset.* If you believe nothing else and use nothing else in this entire book, please remember this. Age is a default negative for many people until and unless it's used in conjunction with power and expertise and confidence. Then it becomes as asset. *This is the pivot point.*

Digression

I believe in and have coined this principle: *Tools for change: The 1 percent solution*®. If you improve by 1 percent a day, in 70 days you're twice as good. That applies to organizations, teams, and people. (Do the math, just keep multiplying 1 times 1 percent 70 times on a calculator and you arrive at 2.)

Not many people do this consistently, or even at all. If you can simply focus on a 1 percent improvement each day, your personal skills, acumen, and resultant power will grow accordingly.

Thus, our personal support system, from the time we are young and as we age, must be one in which we accumulate and steadily expand our expertise and are willing to articulate it and convey it constantly. When people listened to Peter Drucker in his eighties and nineties, they didn't say, "What an old guy to be working in strategy." They said (if they were rational), "What a brilliant man, we're lucky to have met him." People don't listen to Tony Bennett and comment on his age, they comment on his voice and breath control.

As I mentioned at the outset, one of the last bastions of acceptable bias in our society is ageism. No one would dare say today, when offered a candidate for a job, "Is she pretty?" or "What's his religion?" or "Is she gay?" But they often do ask, without hesitation or fear of reaction, "How old is he?" And while, legally, you can't ask a candidate's age, you can generally figure it out from college graduation, appearance, or information on the internet.

The CEOs of Uber and of Fox News had to step down because of sexual harassment issues. Bill O'Reilly lost his job and coveted TV show for the same reason. There is now a Supreme Court case about whether a baker has to provide a cake for the wedding of a gay couple, which is against his belief system. Religious attire is debated for schools. The Pride March took place in New York City while we were there last week.

But what about age? What about ageism? What about the implicit and explicit bias and prejudicial treatment that attends aging? I'm not familiar with that publicity, that court case, that parade.

We advertently and inadvertently feed the ageism bias. A woman at my church, who repeatedly parks in a fire zone illegally, blocking other cars legally parked, is a nuisance. I finally confronted her, and she told me she could park wherever she wanted because she was disabled. I saw nothing wrong with her, but perhaps she had a heart condition, so I said, "In what way?"

"I'm over 65," she said.

"Look inside that church," I replied, "the average age is over 50. Do you think we're all handicapped?"

That's the problem when we accept, let alone seek, special permission, exceptions, and unique circumstances. We think age is somehow a "get out of jail free" card like the ones in Monopoly. But when we use it that way, it's really a "you're not a mainstream person" card.

And that's why we're treated poorly for the error, crime, and/or inevitability of aging.

We have to change that discussion and that reaction. Politely refuse the offer of a seat or early boarding. Don't request or accept a senior discount. Consider donating part or all of your social security payment to charity.

But most of all, assert your talent. On the job, be innovative and creative, as we discussed in the previous chapter. Never take a pass because there's travel or hard work involved. Off the job, volunteer for tough positions, join boards, coach a team, become active in the community.

If you want to be seen as a vibrant force, you have to act like one.

And one final admonition about personal support: We all must keep in shape. There's nothing wrong with pills and doctor's visits for appropriate care. But there's something wrong when we allow our physical condition to deteriorate out of neglect. One of the other allowable biases I alluded to earlier was that of obesity. Heavy, older people are at best seen as jolly; they are not viewed as wise. And at worst they're seen as out of control rather than in control. (I fall down laughing at obese motivational speakers who admonish us to take control of our lives.)

The Community of Your Own Creation

"Community" means "a group of people with common characteristics," which today can be real or virtual. The commonality to which I refer, however, is not age.

It is achievement, excellence, success.

We often find ourselves in communities at work and at home, at play and at school. People tend to migrate toward people like them. Hence, we have gated communities, and urban gentrification, and common entertainment and recreational pursuits. These communities seem to represent common interests and common bonds.

But they don't; they represent stereotypes and decline.

My wife and I visited friends in Florida who live for half the year in a "seniors community." Both are professional people, one retired, one active. All the homes looked alike in this well-manicured compound, and there was a common dining hall in which everyone looked alike. The age demographic was clearly between 55 and 75, and my wife and I were stared at because we were unknown to the well-acquainted, look-alike residents.

"This is strange," said my wife.

"I feel like we're in The Stepford Couples movie," I told her. I couldn't wait to escape.

Contrast that with a dinner in the fine Hollywood restaurant where the Peninsula Hotel concierge had secured a table for my wife, my son, his wife-to-be, and me: Mr. Chang's. Several well-known actors and others in the entertainment business were seated nearby. During the meal, I noticed three very attractive women at a table staring at me. I'm not used to any woman staring at me unless I've spilled my drink on my shirt.

"Are those women staring at me?" I asked my son, who's heavily involved in the entertainment business.

"They certainly are," he confirmed.

"Why would that be?"

"They've never seen you before and are trying to figure out if you're a producer in town or someone else they should get to know."

I immediately said in a loud voice, "So, Jason, let's talk financing for that new project!"

You're familiar with the phrase "You are what you eat"? Well, you are who you hang out with. As I mentioned earlier, my friend and über-coach Marshall Goldsmith was asked once how someone becomes a thought leader.

"You hang out with them," he said immediately. He related how he had literally carried the briefcase of the legendary Peter Drucker, met all of Drucker's acquaintances, and had become friends with them. Now, of course, people try to hang out with Marshall.

Years ago, I realized that people such as Marshall (coaching), Seth Godin (creativity), David Meister (small business growth), Marcus Buckingham (personal development), Walt Mossberg (technology), and others were my peers because of my thought leadership in solo consulting. I began to mention them more often and began hiring authorities and best-selling authors such as Martin Seligman, Robert Cialdini, Dan Pink, Dan Gilbert, and others to speak at my events.

Our ages vary considerably, but we are peers in our respective professions. You don't want to be associated with chronological peers but rather with peers of accomplishment, excellence, and success, with age an irrelevant factor. You want to be regarded as a brilliant person who happens to be 67, not as a 67-year-old who, unbelievably, is still holding his or her own.

That means we create our own communities, real and virtual. A great difficulty for people being promoted to higher-level positions in organizations is that they must really abandon their former peers (who are now subordinates) and embrace their new peers (who were once superiors). That is a hell of a lot more difficult than it sounds! In fact, it's been the objective of a lot of my coaching assignments.

I have colleagues who continue to participate in groups and associations and "mastermind sessions" that they should have long ago abandoned.

Instead of moving on, they are aging with a cohort that has nothing com- mon with them but age and longevity. What are you participating in, sub- scribing to, renewing, and otherwise perpetuating that is more related to your age and past connections than your future and excellence?

One of the things those special senior (and often gated, which is some- what symbolic) communities do is remove youth. Not only do they prohibit children, but activities such as cruises, tours, recreation, and so on are desig- nated for 55 and over or other such arbitrary limits. While there are clearly places for youth in which I'd feel uncomfortable (a deafening hard-rock concert would be one), there are frequent occasions when I'd want youth present ("youth" being people significantly younger than I am).

At work, this means developing a community with people of diverse ages and deliberately striving to understand their perspective. As a solo entrepreneur, it means finding people like yourself who are much younger and offering not to coach them but to befriend them. Socially, it means embracing a wide variety of friends and not migrating to "look-alike" others at events. Within our own families, it means not ignoring comments from someone because of their age or assuming that those of younger generations are not as smart as we are.

Digression

One of my favorite *New Yorker* cartoons was of two people who look exactly alike sitting across a desk from each other, one the interviewer and one the candidate for a job. The former says, "I don't know what it is about you, but I really like you!"

What do we have to master to ensure that we include people from a variety of generations and of different ages in our lives? Here are some suggestions:

- **Stop labeling.** I've discussed this earlier and I raise it again here because once we slap a label on someone, we tend to listen or not listen (or listen selectively) to what they say (just as people are prone to do at times with us). There is no "Greatest Generation" or "Gen Y" prototype. Neither has a lock on the high road.

- **Make yourself into an object of interest.** If you have innovative ideas, are an explorer, provide excellent coaching, take leadership roles, have interesting hobbies, are engaged in the arts, and so forth, people of all ages will tend to approach you. If the only thing you can talk about is your inability to sleep at night, they will not.
- **Join diverse groups.** Service clubs such as the Lions or Elks, the Shriners, and the Knights of Columbus all have an elderly demographic. Join the local Red Cross, or ballet board, or community improvement association. Seek out permanent or temporary organizations that have no particular age appeal.
- **Listen to your kids (or others' kids).** We tend to dismiss our kids (at all ages) as not possibly knowing what we know. But they know a lot that we don't know about contemporary mores and tastes. We overlook this resource the way we often take for granted a beautiful sunset just because we see it every evening. That's a dangerous oversight for both opportunities.[6]

Why Money Is Not Wealth (and What Is)

I can always make another dollar, but I can never make another minute.

Any questions?

That's my philosophy about life. The minute you read the first lines of this chapter or of this segment, that minute was gone. That's why I've focused on experiences as such a critical part of the maturation (and control) process, because we have to build on those times that will never come again.

When my wife and I, newly married, first saw *Fiddler on the Roof* on Broadway, Tevye and Golde have been married for 26 years, and we were both thinking, "What on earth would that be like?" The last time we saw the revival we were married 45 years, 19 years more than Tevye and Golde!

Our perspective had vastly changed relative to the play, its characters, and their situations.

When we were first married, if we'd been asked what makes for a successful, long-term marriage, we would have been guessing. Now we know. When we first started traveling, I kept a list of what I considered great hotels, and one of the first was the Sheraton Waikiki in Honolulu, with its open-air lobby and seaside location. Today, we consider that strictly mid-range and would never stay there. The Sheraton hasn't changed; we have.

We need to capture these fleeting moments and bring them into perspective and, therefore, into *usage*. They are a major aspect of our wisdom. The problem with someone who visited a place many years ago is that their recollections are dated, faded by time; also, the place may have been altered by subsequent events. At one point, Venezuela was a thriving democracy and Colombia was a dangerous place to go. The current situation in these neighboring countries is completely reversed.

Our memories of our experiences are often false. Our inability to go back and linger, barring a working time machine, means that we have to make the absolute best of our current time and use our future time well.

Money, on the other hand, is a continuing, renewable entity. We can earn it at any time if we put our minds to doing so. We can retrieve it from savings. We can invest it to make still more of it. It doesn't disappear of its own inevitable volition; it is ours to create and use, save or spend. Therefore, we can always make more money, but we cannot make another minute.

This brings us to a discussion that not many people understand on their own: Time and money are not resources, *they are priorities*.

We all have 168 hours every week. We know that. How we use and deploy that time is the issue. Some is required for sleep, but people sleep for differing amounts of time. The suggestion to get 8 hours of sleep is simply that—a suggestion. Many people are at their peak with less sleep than that, and some laze in bed until noon. Those are choices.

When people say, "I don't have time to see my kid's soccer game," they are lying. They *do*, obviously, have the time, *but they choose not to use their time to see the game*. That is their right. Perhaps applying that time to making money on the job enables their kid to play soccer in the first place. I make no value judgments. But we have to be honest with ourselves: We *do* have the time, but we choose how to use it.

That's why time is a priority, not a resource. In business, "I don't have time to pursue this project with you" means, in reality, "I choose to use my time in other ways more important to me than pursuing this project with you." Hence, in sales, creating high value and high priority is urgent to have time reassigned.

It's also urgent to have money reassigned. There is always money. The lights are on, the parking lot is plowed, the plants are misted, the bills are paid, the payroll is distributed. There is always money. *The question is how it is used.* "I don't have the budget for this project" means "I don't choose to fund this project with the money I have." When someone does decide to spend money with you, it means "I'm going to give my money to you and not spend it on something else, because I think the work with you is of a higher priority and more important to my well-being."

It's as simple as that.

Both time, which is nonrecoverable, and money, which is collectable, are priorities in terms of how they are spent or not spent. If we want to exert control in the world, we have to remember that the persuasion of, and influence over, others is based on changing how they see the priorities, *and not waiting until a better time or until there is a new budget.* If you wait, you are lost, because other conflicting priorities will appear.

Similarly, you have to decide the priorities for your money and time. We surrender control in many cases because we assign our time and money low priority and spend them on frivolous pursuits instead of on issues vastly more important to us. As we age, there is no requirement, law, regulation, rule, or norm that stipulates we must sacrifice important issues because others deserve them more. There is no necessity to allow others to determine how our time and money are spent.

I've never felt it my obligation to make my children wealthy. I believed my obligation was and is to imbue them with proper values and give them the best education possible, providing love and guidance along the way.

I thought the worst thing would be to enable them in thinking that they always have a safety net and a backstop, so they needn't worry about providing for themselves or managing their lives.

Factoid

If lawmakers don't act, Social Security's trust fund will be tapped out in about 18 years.

That's one takeaway from a recent Social Security and Medicare trustees' annual report.

That doesn't mean retirees will get nothing by 2034. It means that at that point the program will only have enough revenue coming in to pay 79 percent of promised benefits.

So if you're expecting to get $2000 a month, the program will only be able to pay $1580.

Technically, Social Security is funded by two trust funds—one for retiree benefits and one for disability benefits.

The 2034 date is the exhaustion date for both funds when combined. But if considered separately, the old-age fund will be exhausted by 2035, after which it would be able to pay just 77 percent of benefits. And the disability fund will be tapped out by 2023, at which point it could only pay out 89 percent of promised benefits.

To make all of Social Security solvent for the next 75 years would require the equivalent of any of the following: immediately raising the Social Security payroll tax rate to 14.98 percent from 12.4 percent on the first $118,500 of wages, cutting benefits by 16 percent, or some combination of the two.[7]

Before moving to the next chapter, I'll share with you here what *real wealth* is, because it's not money, which is just a renewable fuel source for life. Real wealth is *discretionary time*. Your ability to go where you want, when you want, under the conditions you dictate is true wealth. Most people working in large offices in huge buildings are like prisoners. They can't merely walk out on the street without taking a personal day, a sick day, or a lunch break.

Entrepreneurs theoretically have it better, but many people who are refugees from the business world and go to work for themselves often wind up with a harsher, worse boss! They work ridiculous hours trying to move the gerbil wheel forward instead of in circles.

Our wealth doesn't increase with age just because we have money in the bank. Wealth isn't based on your 401k, IRA, SEP IRA, ROTH IRA, pensions, or savings. Wealth is based on freedom. That's what we should all be pursuing as we mature: freedom.

We don't have freedom if we allow our children to take over our lives because we're "needed" to babysit for two-income families. We don't have freedom if we're told not to spend our money on travel because our children are afraid they'll have to support us if we run out of money. And we don't have freedom if society's norms dictate to us how to live in a dependent and enfeebled manner.

Do I exaggerate? You make that call. Let's look at how much we can seize the day.

Notables

Arthur Rubenstein, 89. Performed a major recital at Carnegie Hall.
P.G. Wodehouse, 93. Wrote his final (97th) novel and was knighted.
Nelson Mandela, 76. Elected president of South Africa.
Mother Teresa, 69. Received the Nobel Peace Prize.
Mahatma Gandhi, 61. Began the Salt March to protest taxes.
Ray Kroc, 59. Became sole owner of McDonald's; active until 82.
William Ivy Baldwin, 82. Walked a tightrope across the Grand Canyon.
Henry Ford, 60. Invented the modern assembly line.

Notes

1. Cleaveland.com, "U.S. life expectancy for 65-year-olds is now to reach age 84.3," http://www.cleveland.com/datacentral/index.ssf/2014/10/us_life_expectancy_for_65-year.html.
2. Don't scoff, a holographic woman provides directions and information at several sites in Boston's Logan Airport at the moment.
3. Pew Research found that 15 percent of the 83.1 million millennials (ages 25–35) are living in their parents' homes, more than any other previous generation at the same age. "Of Interest," *New York Times*, June 22, 2017.
4. John Steinbeck, *The Grapes of Wrath*, Viking Press/James Lloyd, New York, 1939.
5. Understand that I'm always excluding those who deserve special treatment by dint of disability, so this is the last time I'll cite that exception.
6. People born after 1990 have probably never experienced solitaire with actual playing cards, overhead projectors, the whine of a dial-up internet connection, videos from Blockbuster, the Yellow Pages, corded phones, the Dewey Decimal System, album liner notes.
7. Jeanne Sahadi, "Social Security trust fund projected to run dry by 2034," CNN Money, June 22, 2016, http://money.cnn.com/2016/06/22/pf/social-security-medicare/index.html.

CHAPTER 7

Forgiveness Is *Not* Easier Than Simply Appropriating Permission

We deny ourselves based on some real or even imagined societal dictate on what we can do and how we can act, from sexual intimacy to driving, from travel to health care. The way out of this maze is to chop through it and take command of our own lives. We need to stop being victims seeking special treatment (seats reserved for the elderly) and start being independent entrepreneurs creating our own personalized treatment.

The Range of Permissions We Allow and Deny Ourselves

We range from defaulting to a position of powerlessness—no permission—to one of complete autonomy—blanket permission.

The most successful people apply requests for permission situationally and flexibly. There is no "ideal position." One would hope that someone identifying an attacker on an aircraft wouldn't seek permission to leave the seat and try to intervene, or that a doctor encountering an accident wouldn't seek permission to treat the injured.

Conversely, we wouldn't expect people to simply claim what's ours and take our property, or our place in line, or our identity. In fact, we consider those acts criminal in varying degrees.

Have you even been on an airplane shortly after takeoff where, despite smooth flying, the "Fasten seat belt" sign remains on and you need to use the lavatory? You become more and more uncomfortable and hope for the sign to change, but you keep your seat, concerned about a reprimand from flight attendants. You fixate on the sign and wonder if the pilot has forgotten to turn it off.

But then, someone gets up and simply uses the lavatory without any consequences. After that, you (and others) eagerly follow suit. You refused to grant yourself permission but happily accepted the implicit permission granted by someone else (unknowingly).

In Figure 7.1, those on the extreme left (in the eight o'clock position) never have permission. They will stand at the "Don't walk" sign, not moving, even if they can see there is no traffic in either direction for over a mile and it's beginning to pour. Those at the eleven o'clock position wait for others to indicate or tell them it's okay to act, as on the airplane. At one o'clock, we justify our actions to ourselves—"It's unhealthy sitting here with my need to visit the restroom in perfectly smooth air"—before we act. And at four o'clock, we simply act. We don't consider ramifications,

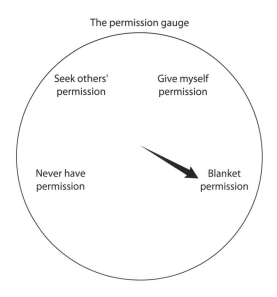

Figure 7.1   *Permission gauge.*

precedent, or others' compliance, we simply act based on our need at the moment.

There are people who raise their hand to speak in meetings and often go unacknowledged for a long time (and/or the subject changes and their point is no longer relevant) and those who merely speak out when they have something to say.

Digression

There are actually coaches and models that suggest you dress and behave similarly to those you want to impress. Perhaps that's why many people claim they begin to resemble their dogs at some point.

The proper balance is probably somewhere between those last two positions, say three o'clock, depending on the situation and the urgency. Blanket permission wouldn't include cutting the line at a theater or train station, for example. But speaking out in a meeting is often important.

The extremes are fairly easy to identify (though not always, since doctors have been sued for giving unsolicited help to accident victims and cutting the line is seen nightly at New York theaters). It's the *range* of our choices that is important to exploit.

We do what we're told at TSA checkpoints and when the police are directing traffic. We use our initiative in unusual situations. In the horrible London fire in an apartment building in June 2017, many of the people who perished were following the orders of the building's fire brigade, which turned out to be ill-advised.

In a famous psychological experiment, a group of houseflies was placed in a large jar with the bottom against a window and the open end facing the room. A group of bees was placed in similar conditions. The scientists believed that the bees would emerge first, since they're known to be more intelligent than houseflies.

However, all the flies, merely flying in random patterns, escaped. The bees all died because they clustered near the light source, believing it was the way out. Like the bees, who stuck to logic, we don't always fare well if we feel compelled to toe the line.

We often need permission to avoid what seems like the obvious or logical. Chesley Sullenberger famously landed his aircraft, with no loss of life, in the Hudson River after a collision with geese shut down both engines of his passenger jet. Many "experts" felt he should have tried to get back to the airport. He didn't need permission to do what he felt was best and was, unarguably, the best course of action. The experts would have been wrong.

As we age, we seem to seek permission more *when we should be granting ourselves permission more*. I'm not talking about anarchy, law-breaking, disrespect, or indifference. I'm talking about using our wisdom and experience to dictate where we should be on that permission gauge in any given circumstance. We shouldn't be "making way" for others because we're older, we should be setting the way for others.

In organizations, institutional memory is vital, and in families, lore is often profound. Embodied in both are the shortcuts, circumventions, and express lanes around certain burdensome permissions as well as the judgment and wisdom to observe required permissions.

"Forgiveness is easier than permission" is an excuse. We don't need excuses, we need the judgment to know when to give ourselves permission for the common good and for our own good.

Removing Fear

Fear is an emotion. Logic causes people to think, but emotion prompts them to act. Consequently, fear is hugely powerful because it generally creates a "fight or flight" response. But I would add another element to that classic psychological definition: "fright."

Fear directly affects our ability to perform, no less than a mental illness such as clinical depression or a physical illness such as arthritis. It masks talent, preventing you from realizing your true abilities. Fear is a basic survival mechanism embedded in us, but it's one no longer based on a creature threatening our survival but rather on a range of often superficial, modern concerns. *Constant fear is incapacitating.* If we become more fearful as we age, we become more incapacitated, despite our physical health.

The results of fear include

- Slowing or stopping functions not needed for survival. One example would be the digestive system, which is why people have intestinal problems when in such a state.
- Blood flow increases, so that our heart rate increases, which creates the sensation of our hearts pounding in our chests, and cardiovascular damage can result.
- Immune systems are weakened. Accelerated aging can occur.
- Memory function is adversely affected, and we lose perspective, which exaggerates the fear we're feeling.
- Decision-making and critical thinking skills are interrupted, so that we miss social cues and often react impulsively.

Note that these are not symptoms of aging but symptoms of *fear*.

Clinical depression can result from chronic fear. Yet our fears today are not basically those caused by threats to our survival but rather by *threats to our egos*. Our egos shouldn't "age." That is, they should be intact and constant. These three possible reactions to fear are hugely negative.

1. **Fight.** This is a survival instinct, often irrational because the issue isn't worth fighting over. It's the basis of road rage, where a perceived, and often unintended, slight on the highway results in injury or even death. *Too many people walk around in a sort of "life rage."*

2. **Fright.** This is a state of indecisiveness and vacillation caused by a reluctance to act at all, to either fight or flee. It is immobilizing. We've seen stage fright, where people freeze during a speech or presentation. The perceived threat is certainly not to their survival but rather to their ego.

3. **Flight.** This is the tendency to physically or emotionally and psychologically run away. We refuse to deal with the issue. We don't show up or we refuse to engage. Children holding their hands over their ears and shouting so as not to hear bad news are examples of flight, even though they haven't gone anywhere.

Let's return to our focus on finding *cause* as an aspect of our critical thinking skills. What are the causes of fear as we mature in our modern times?

- **Being wrong.** We become obsessed with being culpable, of making an error, as if it's a sign of decline. Yet if we aren't failing, we aren't trying. *Innovation can only succeed if there's the freedom to fail.* We have to change our metric that indicates an error is a failure and a failure is a negative. An error is human and a failure is a learning experience.

- **Being criticized.** Right or wrong, everything is public today and everyone is entitled to be a critic. We have to become accustomed to the reactions and *refuse to pay attention to unsolicited feedback.* On the internet, these dispensers of negative critique are called "trolls," and for good reason. Accept critique from people you respect and have consulted, and ignore the rest.

- **Being inappropriate.** We worry about not being hip or with the in-crowd. We worry about what we're wearing or our language or what fork to use. If you're uncertain, get help with your wardrobe, speaking, or table manners. These are learnable skills that, once mastered, provide great confidence.

Digression

Having made a keynote speech for a national association in Manchester, England, I was swept into a reception. Sure enough, within 90 seconds, a man approached me, informed me he was a speech coach, and wanted to give me feedback.

"When you move around the stage," he informed me, "I can't focus well on the points you're making. But when you stand in one spot, I can focus exactly on your point. Do you know what that's called?"

"Yes," I told him, "a learning disability."

- **Being challenged.** This is part of the "imposter syndrome," in which our lack of self-esteem creates the false notion that someone out there is smarter and more experienced and is just waiting to undermine our points and embarrass us in public. That is akin to the monster-under-the-bed belief. You cannot empirically prove there's never been a monster down there, but you can point out that you've never encountered one, nor has anyone else.
- **Being a "loser."** Our quest for perfection (rather than merely success or excellence) creates a profoundly mistaken impression that life is a win/lose, pass/fail kind of game. It is not. Perfection is the killer of excellence. To be fearful of imperfection is to fear life itself. No airplane ride, dinner, theatrical performance, or automobile drive you've ever experienced has been "perfect," yet the experience was fine.

Here is the critical belief you need to embrace to prevent fear from causing you to underperform, acting in ways that are inappropriate and unrepresentative of your talents: *Healthy people want you to succeed, and most people are healthy.*

Never begin with the supposition that the other person is somehow "damaged." It's amazing how many salespeople and entrepreneurs, for example, immediately assume that the prospect or investor in front of them is somehow at fault or flawed, *when they have, in fact, been smart enough to engage in a business conversation with them!* Every audience you face, whether around a conference table or in an auditorium, wants you to succeed, because only people with a personality disorder want to say to others, "I had a great morning, wasted 2 hours watching someone bore us and make a fool of himself." Are there such people? Sure, perhaps about 5 percent of the population, so why not focus on the healthy 95 percent?

We need to stop being afraid. Age should provide calmness and perspective, not increased fears. When people today talk of terrorism, I recall the Cuban Missile Crisis when I was in high school, when many people thought the entire world was going to blow up.

Here's comedian Jerry Seinfeld: "Apparently, people fear public speaking more than death. So the guy delivering the eulogy is more frightened than the guy in the casket."

It is that silly.

Extirpating Guilt

Guilt is different from fear but just as deadly. Fear is often anticipated, while guilt often comes after the fact. Ironically, perhaps, as we mature we have seen more and fear less (there are no monsters under the bed; it's safe to eat the food; flying isn't all that bad), yet we have more experiences and thus more guilt (I should have said "I'm sorry" before he died; I don't deserve my success because my sister didn't have my options; I wasn't there when friends needed me).

Guilt is now so prevalent that it's become a verb: We talk about "guilting" people, as in "We guilted her into chairing the fundraising drive." That's because we've come to realize that guilt can promote certain behaviors and inhibit others.

Because we can accumulate guilt as we age—and often with no way to atone for what we perceive as our fault—it can collect like barnacles on a ship's hull and slow the speed or even cripple the vessel. Picture sclerosis of tissue or plaque on teeth. These are all ailments, except that sclerosis can be medically alleviated and plaque scraped off; guilt tends to cling forever because we don't seek help getting rid of it.

Guilt is the fact of having committed an offense (or crime) by omission or commission. It is also a feeling of having done wrong. It almost always involves hurting someone else (if it were merely personal, it would most likely be considered "sin" by those who are religious). The key is that low self-esteem magnifies guilt and high self-esteem puts it in the proper perspective.

We feel guilty when

- **We've let others down.** We made the error in the business transaction, the ballgame, or the choice of vacation spots that resulted in a bad deal, a lost game, or a disappointing trip.
- **We didn't intervene when we should have.** We didn't provide more training for the new underwriter, didn't talk intimately enough to our kids about drinking and driving, didn't ask the resort for a better room, so the underwriter was fired, our kid was in an accident, and we had no ocean view.
- **We acted selfishly.** We lobbied for the business trip to Europe, bought a car that our partner had doubts about and didn't like, and insisted on our favorite restaurant, so that colleagues resented our trip, our partner won't use the car, and our friends on restricted diets had to order salads.
- **We don't feel we deserve what we have (imposter syndrome).** Others were laid off work while we held our jobs; we received a small inheritance from a distant relative; we were upgraded to first class. We ask why we were chosen and not others. We did nothing to earn the reward or benefit.
- **Others make us feel guilty.** Parents are great at this ("You never call me"). Kids are quite good at it ("You embarrass me picking

me up at school since you won't get me a car"). Colleagues are adept at it ("Who do you know to get the prime office?"). Society at large creates this pressure. At TSA checkpoints in airports, we're guilty until proven innocent. They ensure you don't have banned materials before you can proceed; they don't take your word for it. Banks have cameras focused on customers at all times. (In fact, there are more surveillance cameras in our society right now than at any other time—more than a quarter billion in the world.[1])

- **Collective guilt.** We're told we should feel responsible for climate change, world hunger, animal welfare, racial conflict. There are empty phrases used by various interests—often legitimate interests—to gain support.

Let's stop here. There are plenty of sources of guilt, and they accumulate and accrete as we age, the stalagmites and stalactites of our conscience.

And these sources obviously grow as we do. Family and others won't let them go. We don't release them but keep adding to them. We are loaded down by increasing guilt that we can't seem to shed or lighten. One of the potentially fatal aspects of threescore and more is the physical, mental, and emotional stress created by unmitigated and unrelieved guilt.

So let's get rid of it.

Here are the steps you can take today and utilize every day to avoid, manage, atone for, and ultimately jettison guilt. Remember, there is nothing positive about guilt, it is a totally negative and draining emotion.

1. **Recognize it.** Say, "I feel guilty about…" Then ask yourself if it's truly your fault. Someone else being laid off is not your fault. Ask if there was truly something rational you did or didn't do to create the situation causing your guilt. Dismiss those that occurred independent of your action or inaction. You have nothing to feel guilty about if you

don't have time to volunteer to clean the park, but you do if you throw your garbage in the park.

2. **Separate guilt from accountability.** Pointing out someone's error, unethical behavior, or sloppiness so that others are not harmed by it is responsible behavior. Grounding your kid for violating rules or failing to do promised work is good parenting. We all have to make accountable decisions at work and in society.

3. **Where you are responsible for a thoughtless or hurtful act, apologize.** The best way to apologize is in person (including Skype or Zoom at the moment). Accept responsibility, say the words "I'm deeply sorry," and ask if there's anything else you can do. (Most of the time, when you ask others what will improve a situation, they ask for less than you would have offered on your own.) Then move on. You did what you had to and you can't continue to hold onto it. If the other person rejects your apology, that is his or her right, *but there's nothing more to be done.*

4. **Never enable "guilters."** I know someone who is highly successful and wealthy, but his mother asks him to drive her personally to a distant airport despite the fact that he can provide a car service and she is not incapacitated in any way. He drives her every time, and she keeps insisting he do it. If he refused, she would either accept the car service or miss her flight. Which do you think would happen?

5. **Learn your lesson.** The positive thing about guilt and dealing with it successfully is that you avoid it in the future by changing your behavior when required. You don't insist on your restaurant. You find a compromise about the car. You inquire more thoroughly before your trip.

6. **Adjust what you can, forget what you can't.** You can't take back a throwing error in a ball game. If you let it haunt you, the odds are that you'll make another one. But you can alter your vacation if you find you're having a bad time, and you can return a poorly chosen gift and find a better one with the recipient's advice.

A clinician reminded me once that a total absence of guilt is one of the traits of a sociopath! I'm not arguing here for refusal to accept guilt or recognize it. I am strongly suggesting that the effort to rid yourself of it and prevent it in the future is an important part of retaining control and power at threescore and beyond.

The New *Carpe Diem*

If we ignore the normative pressures and social dictates about aging and decide to act and behave as we deem appropriate for ourselves (and not our chronology), we can set our own path. We escape the crazy maze that says, "You are here," but there's no way to "get over there." Instead, we chop through the bushes.

Consider these ideas your machete.

Japan has the highest proportion of people over 65 in the workforce today among the Group of Seven Industrial Nations, at 22.8 percent.[2] The United States is second, with 19.3 percent. In Japan, more than a quarter of the population is over 65 and the government is concerned about how to provide support for these people. Consequently, they are encouraging companies to retain older employees and even paying bonuses to do so.

The concept that older, high-priced employees are past their prime and can be replaced with less expensive, younger people has failed to be validated. Especially in sales, for example, employees with long histories of developing key clients and customers—and with thousands of names and relationships in the marketplace—are almost irreplaceable. In an appreciation of this dynamic, Pola Orbis Holdings has 1500 salespeople in their seventies to nineties. Daiwa Securities Group has scrapped its mandatory retirement age of 70. The firm's CEO, Seiji Nakata, said, "This will make it possible for us to have more consultants in the age range of 60–80, *which is similar to the generation that holds the largest financial assets.*" (Emphasis mine.)

Digression

Shigekazu Miyazaki retired from All Nippon Airways, the country's largest, at the mandatory age of 65. But today, he's flying for Oriental Air Bridge. "I'm healthy, and I love to fly, so why not do so as long as I can?" he commented to reporters.

With the longest life expectancy, a shrinking population (births have fallen under one million for the first time since measuring began in 1899), and near zero unemployment—accompanied by the discouragement of immigration—Japan faces a demographic crisis. More than half the country's taxi drivers are over 60 and less than 10 percent of the population is under 40.[3]

"Seizing the day" is not only good advice, it's going to be mandatory for people in businesses, entrepreneurs, solo practitioners, part-time workers, and others who seek to remain vital. Despite the *fact* of the worth of mature people and their contributions, the prevailing sentiment, reflected (or, perhaps, created by) the media is not consistent with that reality.

Here's a typical piece of reporting on President George H. W. Bush and his wife, who were in their favorite vacation place, Kennebunkport, Maine. In what was meant to be a complimentary piece on the Bushes' love for the place and the locals' reciprocal sentiments, the reporter feels obligated to write—and this appeared in the teaser on the web site along with the headline—"Despite the frailties of age—the 41st president has been hampered by vascular parkinsonism, which mimics Parkinson's disease, and Barbara has begun riding a motorized scooter—the couple seem to be everywhere in Kennebunkport."[4]

It's as if it's a miracle that the Bushes can enjoy themselves, or as if the reporter thinks the town's receptivity is based on some incapacity. We've come a long way from the times when President Franklin Roosevelt's inability to walk due to polio was hidden from the general public with the complicity and agreement of the media. There were whispers when he ran for governor that his health was a major drawback. He eventually was elected president four times and saw the country successfully through all but the very end of World War II.

Can you imagine today someone talking about a CEO's, celebrity's, or athlete's life and business with such qualifiers about his or her health? Aside from the scandal publications, the media is very circumspect. After all, a young person's career could be ruined. The person might sue. Investors, fans, and supporters might be outraged. Apparently, it's fine to talk about ailments when the subject is older, but not younger. We expect it when people are older, and we expect that they are in the process of falling apart anyway!

That's why we have to knock the stereotypes down and protest this kind of blatant bias with our positive behaviors. How do you seize the day, in light of these prejudices?

- Don't accept any reference to talent diminished simply because of age. I talked earlier of my letter to the *New York Times* protesting an insensitive reviewer's (a woman, no less) offhanded dismissal of Tom Wolfe's work as the result of his being "an old man." The *Times* had sense enough to print the letter. Stop someone midsentence if he or she is in your presence or write if he or she is not. These throwaway lines about age are detrimental and damaging.

- Talk about your age, don't hide it. We've become afraid that we'll be dismissed or disqualified if we own up to our actual age. People omit it from résumés (as if in so doing it's impossible to determine). We say "mature" or "senior" or "older" or use some other euphemism. "I'm in my seventies" is not accurate; "I'm 74" is accurate. When the media delicately reports "a woman of indeterminate years," it's an insult, not a compliment.

- Stop talking about illnesses. I've heard the same person talk about the same illness in every single conversation, irrespective of whether the others have already heard it. (They have.) By all means, seek advice, and use your support system if you need to talk. But your physical ailments shouldn't be the topic of the day unless you're on your deathbed, and you'll get there that much faster if you talk only of your illnesses.

- Take up new interests. You don't have to skydive or kite sail (although many older people have), but it's never too late to learn about art, fine wine, music, theater, history, or meditation. Don't do this with specific groups sorted by age! Do so with people of all ages. You don't age by being active, physically and/or mentally, you age by being *inactive*. To be an object of interest to others, you must have intense interests yourself.

- Stay informed. Use modern technology. Never say, "I don't need this in my position." In your business, hobbies, and personal life, use all means to communicate and to learn. Take online courses. One of the worst replies I know of—and deadly at all ages when diverse groups form—is, "Oh, I don't follow that."

- Coach younger people. In my 30-plus years of consulting, I've learned the most when teaching and coaching others. For many years, it was older executives; then it was peers; now it's mostly younger people. The learning is the same; it doesn't diminish. Coach in your business specialty, your private interests, finance, sports, and so forth. There is a genuine reciprocity in coaching, because they and you both need and profit from the experience. If you really want to learn something, try to coach others in it.

We need to stop seeking forgiveness, stop asking permission, and stop expecting favors and exceptions. If you want to seize the day, assume permission. Stop being afraid and stop feeling guilty. Apologize for the mistakes that we all make, which are completely unrelated to age, and move on. Don't see yourself as a victim who should seek special treatment. That seat on some trains and airport trams that says, "Reserved for seniors" is not for you.

Notables

In 2017, at the age of 39, Tom Brady, the quarterback of the New England Patriots, won his fifth Super Bowl. In breaking the previous record of four, he led his team back from a 25-point deficit. The previous Super Bowl record for recovering from a deficit was 10 points. He did this with two touchdowns in the fourth quarter, each followed by a difficult two-point conversion to tie the game, and then won the game on the first possession in overtime.

In so doing, he broke eight records and tied a ninth. Many sports authorities consider this the most dramatic comeback in the history of any professional sport, and almost everyone considers him to be the best quarterback to ever play. The Patriots are favored to win again in 2018, when Brady will still be the quarterback at 40. He says he wants to play eight more years.

Why do I note Tom Brady, who, while remarkable, was hardly near threescore when he did this? Because there have only been seven quarterbacks in history who played at his age, and none was nearly as good. In fact, none was close. Nor are quarterbacks playing today in their twenties and thirties.

Brady's ability to look at a defense and instantly recognize its weaknesses, and call the proper play to exploit it, is based on his athletic maturity. He *is* "threescore and more" in his chosen field, and he's at the top of his game.

Notes

1. Niall Jenkins, "245 Million Video Surveillance Cameras Installed Globally in 2014," IHS Markit, June 11, 2015, https://technology.ihs.com/532501/245-million-video-surveillance-cameras-installed-globally-in-2014.

2. These and the facts that follow from Megumi Fujikawa, "More Older Workers Aren't Shy about Not Retiring," *Wall Street Journal*, July 3, 2017.
3. Jonathan Soble, "The Pilot in the Cockpit? In Japan, He Might Be a Retiree," *New York Times*, July 31, 2017.
4. Brian MacQuarrie, "Kennebunkport Loves the Bush Family, and the Feeling Is Mutual," *Boston Globe*, July 3, 2017.

CHAPTER 8

Eliminating Scarcity in Your Soul

The key to powerful aging is powerful growth. The laws of entropy erode plateaus, so we must keep advancing and climbing, which is an alien concept to many because our society doesn't think it appropriate past a certain age. These are the four critical areas to healthy growth that need ongoing attention and development.

Physical Health

As I mentioned at the outset, although average lifespans have gradually lengthened over generations, it was not unusual for the ancient Greeks to live into their seventies and beyond. In Japan today, the average age is 85, and in Iceland it's 83, while many African nations still have lifespans only into the fifties.[1]

Contributing factors are heredity (possibly the strongest), nutrition, weight, habits (e.g., smoking), diet, and employment (logging and fishing and are more dangerous than insurance underwriting). *Yet even here, we find that the Japanese use tobacco far more than do Americans, yet have longer average lifespans by about 6 years.*

Our physical condition determines what kinds of jobs we can do, for how long, to what degree, and how safely. Something as mundane as a plane trip can be serious for those with poor circulation or obesity. High blood pressure limits the amount of stress one can endure. Poor eyesight or hearing will decrease work options.

An important aspect of physical health is that some major concerns are being better addressed than relatively minor ones. I was impressed, for example, while at Hewlett-Packard, watching a woman park a van using hand controls in a modified vehicle, then lowering her wheelchair to the ground, closing the doors remotely, and easily entering the building to go to work. Wheelchair ramps are ubiquitous. Many people (healthy and otherwise) are able to work from home for major companies. Airlines and hotels are adept at accommodating people with disabilities who travel for work or personal reasons.

However, it's tougher when your incapacity is less severe but nonetheless difficult for productivity. When you are diabetic, arthritic, or obese, or have emphysema, migraines, poor muscle tone, and so on, life can be extremely difficult. The uncomfortable truth is that the workplace, social spaces, entertainment, restaurants, and so forth do not easily accommodate these conditions.

Digression

When I was in my late forties, there were no rolling bags for travel. Businesspeople tended to carry a large fold-over garment bag or small suitcase along with a briefcase (and a pocketbook or tote bag for women) through the airport.

I was changing planes in Chicago with a long distance between gates, and found myself huffing and puffing, trying to catch my breath. I was seriously out of shape, though I didn't look it. But that day I became disgusted with myself over something I could personally control.

I joined a gym and worked out three times a week. But I soon began cheating, not doing the exercises properly or doing them too fast or skipping the tougher ones. My improvement was minimal.

My wife had a personal trainer, so I enrolled at that gym. Within a month, I was no longer huffing and puffing, and I felt better than ever. My weight barely changed, but my stamina and endurance did. Twenty years later, I still go three times a week when I'm not traveling. Here's the key: I hate it; I don't enjoy it at all. They tell you that endorphins are released that improve your health, but I must be endorphinless.

Nonetheless, I complete every exercise the trainers assign, and I'm told I'm in better shape than most people 20 years younger.

You know what your heredity is. If there is cancer or heart problems or clinical depression or alcoholism in your family, you have to be highly alert for the signs and be willing to take the preventive actions. You also know what your environment is, at work and at home. You have to be sensitive to stressors, dangers, and unhealthy conditions. You also know your own habits and interests. You have to be sensitive to what is prudent (skiing or scuba diving with instruction) and foolish (smoking three packs of cigarettes a day).

Note that I keep saying "you." This is not a government responsibility or a social agency focus. We have to be accountable for our own health and lives. If you choose to ignore medical advice and follow rumors on social media for treatment, that is your decision—and not a good one.

Frankly, it is far easier to impress others and to be successful when you are healthy. Aside from incapacitating illnesses, accidents, and disease, here's what will keep you healthy and, therefore, impressive and successful:

- **Diet.** Find out what actually works for you in terms of weight, cholesterol, blood pressure, and other metrics. Eschew faddish diets. (The current gluten-free craze is only relevant if one has celiac disease, for example. Otherwise, it's merely an affectation.) A good diet differs from person to person based on physiology and metabolism. Stick with an effective regimen.

- **Visit your doctor.** Although the worth of annual physicals is often debated (as is, for example, prostate cancer checks or mammograms), I've found that a twice-yearly visit at threescore and more serves to quickly address any nascent problems and monitor existing ones effectively. Both my father and uncle had diabetes, but I've managed to avoid it with a single daily pill.
- **Visit the gym (or equivalent).** Exercise on a regular basis. There's no question about its positive benefits. If you're highly disciplined, you can do so on your own—running, power walking, training with weights, biking, hiking, swimming, and so forth. If you're like me, undisciplined and resistant, you need a trainer focused on you, not a gym you can get lost in.
- **Visit the dentist.** Gum diseases and bad dental hygiene are prime causes of disease and poor health. Get your teeth cleaned and examined twice a year.
- **Give up bad habits.** You can stop smoking, drink less, change your caloric intake, and get more sleep if needed. You may need a counselor or a coach, but what you don't need is to be a martyr by working long hours, living on junk food, and being in a constant frazzle. (The humorist George Ade once said, "Don't pity the martyrs, they love the work.")

Lesson

I was sitting in first class on the Acela high-speed train heading to New York from Providence next to a man of about my age. At one point he took out a small toiletry kit and went back to the restroom. I hardly noticed, and when I looked up from my keyboard, he had returned.

A minute later, a woman approached him, scolding him, "You were in that lavatory for 10 minutes shaving," she admonished, "and that is selfish and completely unacceptable!"

"I was in there for just a few minutes, and I wasn't shaving," he mildly replied.

"Don't lie to me," she yelled, "I saw your shaving kit!"

"That was my insulin kit, I'm diabetic, and it was time for an injection," he said.

"Well, you *still* took too long!" she steamed as she departed.

Some people are totally unforgiving, and we can't help them. But we can help ourselves.

Let's take a look at why an often underappreciated panoply of health is so important in supporting the other aspects of a healthy existence.

Emotional Health

I'll repeat an earlier admonition: Logic influences us to think; emotion influences us to act. All emotions are valid, in that they are accurate reflections of one's mood, temperament, and circumstances at the time. While another person may find them inappropriate, that is irrelevant, because they are real for the individual experiencing them. As opposed to facts, logic, and intellectualism, emotions are often intuitive and instinctual; they are usually (but not always) personal and not shared.

Because emotions produce actions, it's vital to be emotionally healthy.

Success, it may seem, should make people happy. But it's actually the reverse: Happy people tend to be more successful than unhappy people. Therefore, the state of your emotional health is quite vital as you mature and, for that matter, for anyone who wants to thrive. Emotionally happy people are more likely to work toward legitimate and important goals, find and attract the skills, talents, and resources required for success, and maintain optimistic views of life. Their resilience is stronger because of these traits.

Ask yourself these questions as indicators of your emotional health:

- Are you in control of your thoughts, attitudes, and resultant behaviors under all conditions? Or do you tend to do things and say things you regret afterward?
- Do you look at surprises, obstacles, and resistance as challenges and positives or as setbacks and undermining factors? Emotionally healthy people see questions from others not as threats but rather as signs of interest and opportunities.
- Do you recover quickly from setbacks, taking corrective action? Or are you thrown and require assistance and/or excessive time to recover?
- Do you manage negative feelings well? Emotionally healthy people are not immune to anger, stress, and resentment but can handle these conditions positively.
- Do you seek help when a problem or condition is more than you can manage yourself? That is healthy, whether you consult a partner, coach, or therapist. There are some things we can't cope with alone and the emotional stability to accept such help is vital.

This may sound counterintuitive, but creating and sustaining emotional health is a *skill*. Managing emotional health successfully is complementary to maintaining good physical health. Poor emotional health directly affects blood pressure, weight gain and loss, stress, and heart disease, among other conditions.

Your emotional well-being will dictate your proper behavior and responses at work, as well as with family and friends. As we mature, people mistakenly believe that our emotional reactions are more severe and troublesome. In fact, experience and the skills to manage emotions are usually sharper and more refined. Here are some skills-builders:

- **Be aware.** Identify your emotional responses as opposed to your intellectual responses. A therapist will tell you, "I didn't ask what you *think* about the issue, I asked what you *felt* about it."

- **Be appropriate.** Express your feelings in honest, candid discussion, not in outbursts. But do express them, because repressed anger, for example, or unshared sadness can create high stress levels.
- **Create purpose for your life.** We mistakenly think that we should search for purpose, when in fact we need to create it for ourselves. Volunteer, coach, contribute—do what you find rewarding for others and you reward yourself emotionally.
- **Understand you have only one life.** There is no such thing as a work life and a personal life. They are one. Trying to "balance" them is ridiculous; they are not compartmentalized. Emotional issues in one area of life directly influence the other.
- **Reinforce reciprocity by caring for and improving your physical well-being.** This involves both exercise and environment. Create a healthy diet and eliminate bad habits. Make your environment as happy and peaceful as possible.
- **Think before you take action.** *It's not what happens to you, it's what you do about it.* This is why road rage is such an issue, as people react without thinking while driving a deadly weapon. Too many people walk around with "life rage."
- **Manage your stress, and seek help if you need it.** No one should try to eliminate stress, since positive stress (eustress) keeps adrenaline flowing and enables high performance, especially under pressure. But consult a doctor or therapist if you are unable to deal with excessive stress.
- **Stay connected communally.** We need others, not isolation, and not solely family. Find kindred spirits. Engage.
- **Periodically review your emotional health.** Take some time to think about how you've tended to handle setbacks (or even trauma and crisis) at work and at home. Ask yourself if you've used your maturity and experience intelligently to cope with these issues.

As you can see in Figure 8.1, a moderate amount of stress leads to peak performance. When stress is too low, productivity is low because people

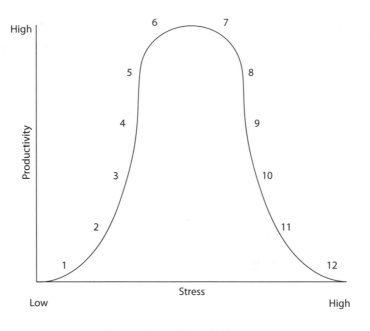

Figure 8.1   *Stress bell curve.*

have no incentive to make things happen, and when stress is too high, people are too scared to act.

Hence, emotionally, we need moderate stress levels to perform at our best. But bear in mind at all times the secret of true emotional health: It is the ability to understand the reality that what happens to us is one thing, but what we choose to do about it is the critical thing. We can't simply act on our emotions, we must use them in conjunction with rationality and objectivity. That capability requires effective psychological health.

Psychological Health

Psychological tests today purportedly identify behavioral predispositions, tendencies to act, personality traits, and so forth. But the fact is, most are merely horoscopes in their predictive ability. They provide such generic and broad descriptions that the individual is bound to find accurate descriptors, or they assign people to quadrants where they supposedly, psychologically, reside.

Licensed therapists are certified to administer certain tests, but even these often yield questionable results. Historically, one of the most popular tests administered by professionals has been the Minnesota Multiphasic Personality Inventory. Yet that test was originally devised in the 1940s to test whether farmers and rural people were mentally healthy enough to serve in the armed forces. It was meant to determine fitness or non-fitness—pass or fail—and not to identify particular traits or degrees of mental health.

It was not a rheostat, but an "off/on" switch.

Today, we have commercial tests that can be administered by nearly anyone with a modicum or training or no training at all. They are often commercial successes, reaping revenue from corporations and individuals, but are highly unreliable and seldom scientifically validated. The Myers–Briggs Type Indicator®, for example, was originally developed by a Pennsylvania housewife who had no psychological or scientific background at all. Instruments such as DISC, which enables consultants to charge more for their services by buying it at x and selling it at $x+$, is based on concepts created by William Moulton Marston in the 1920s. Marston, a psychologist, also created the first polygraph test and the cartoon character Wonder Woman.

Many of these tests are "forced choice," meaning you must select one answer of four provided, even though it may not be exactly right or two might seem equal. There is a large measure of error in forced choice tests, and the repeat reliability (the chance that taking the test repeatedly will yield the same results) is not high.

Finally, these instruments are often used to label and "explain away" people, rather than understand them. Phrases such as

- What do you expect from a high assertive?
- You're not going to persuade an INTJ.
- You're dealing with a dominant personality.

are often only thin substitutes for

- What do you expect from a woman?
- You can't argue with someone from that background.
- *What do you expect from someone his age?*

The first set of descriptors, based on test "results," are often merely conscious or unconscious biases actually reflecting the second set of statements, which I hope we'd all find abhorrent, though far too common.[2]

With physical health, we often have a healthy organ or other body part to compare with the unhealthy one. That's not as easily done in psychological health. We know what a healthy bone or heart looks like, but do we know what a healthy psychological state looks like?

The World Health Organization's definition: "a state of well-being in which [an] individual realizes his or her own potential, can cope with normal stresses of life, can work productively and fruitfully, and is able to contribute to his or her community."[3]

I don't believe our psychological health is determined by tests, especially those administered by unqualified people using instruments not validated to accurately determine results! I believe that flexibility is the key to successful human interaction, not residence in a box, quadrant, or nest that must be identified and adjusted to by others. Here are some guidelines for you to consider in gauging your personal health in this area.

- Do I behave ethically, with a consistent sense of right and wrong?
- Do I operate in the real world and not one of fantasy, and would others concur with my reality?
- Do I have a relatively accurate self-view, consistent with the way in which others would describe me?
- Am I able to create, sustain, and enjoy relationships of both long and short duration?
- Am I resilient to the degree that I can recover from most setbacks rapidly and completely?

- Do I curtail my emotional reactions so that my manifest behavior is constructive and well received?
- Is my view of others accurate in that it is shared by most third parties?
- Do I avoid excessive guilt and blame, and apologize and atone appropriately when required?
- Do I deal with fear intelligently and sensibly rather than default to a fight or flight alternative?

As you can see, these are derived from most of the subjects we've discussed in the book thus far. There is no perfect psychological state, but there is a continuum of healthy states, and positive reactions to the questions above place you in a very healthy position on it.

Digression

I was asked to be an expert witness in a case where a Fortune 100 company had two employees, one a human resources representative and another an engineer, administer a third-party test to an executive who was being considered for promotion to CEO. The test results and their analysis indicated he wasn't right for the job behaviorally and psychologically, and he was passed over, effectively ending his career.

He left, declined severance, and sued. His lawyer and I went through two depositions at a very expensive New York law firm with all the resources in the world. They had a psychologist who was a professional expert witness; that was all he did.

I testified that it was extremely and unquestionably unethical to use a nonvalidated test (for these purposes) administered and interpreted by two lay people to make any kind of assessment at all about anyone. The defense was blistering in their rebuttal and questioning.

And then they settled, handsomely, out of court. There's just no question that these approaches do more damage than good.

Intellectual Health

As we age, our intellect should remain sharp. There is scientific evidence of physiological changes that are unseen; for example, lung capacity decreases in most cases. But there is no evidence that intellectual decline is inevitable. You can see that among the "Notables" I've included at the chapter conclusions.

We've all heard that playing word games, doing crossword puzzles, engaging in memorization, and practicing other techniques can help people retain intellectual acuity. My personal formula has been massive reading and writing. I discussed earlier the importance of language, for example, and healthy debate keeps one sharp.

However, let's look at intellectual health and power from a pragmatic standpoint, not an abstract one. What is it that we can do, specifically, at work and at home to strengthen and sustain intellectual power? I believe that there is a sequence involved that can be learned and applied in virtually all situations.

If you recall the discussion on wisdom and how it accrues with the experiences of many years, you can see how it is naturally associated with maturity. But it's difficult to simply hit the switch and "be wise"! There's a lot of pressure when people turn to you and expect that you can cut through the vagaries and the ambiguity and provide clarity and direction.

I deconstructed what we actually do when we're successful in being wise. It looks like this:

In Figure 8.2, I've labeled the box on the left as the fuel tanks. These contain the propellant that enables you to accelerate at any time. They are, in detail

- **Recognition of success.** Knowing when you've met or exceeded goals and why, so that you can replicate the process without reinventing the wheel each time. *It's more important to know WHY you're good than THAT you're good.*

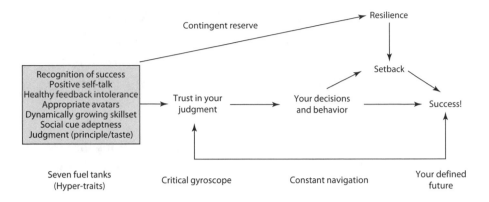

Figure 8.2 *The wisdom process.*

- **Positive self-talk.** This is the psychological healthy step of generalizing your victories and isolating your defeats, and looking at obstacles as challenges to be overcome and not problems that will sink you.
- **Healthy feedback intolerance.** We should listen to those we respect and have asked for advice, and not be battered like a ball in a pinball machine by every random piece of feedback (almost all of which is to benefit the sender, not you).
- **Appropriate avatars.** Who are the exemplars we most admire, and how can we emulate the traits that cause us to hold them in such esteem?
- **A dynamically growing skill set.** We should be learning daily through our efforts, our coaching of others, our investment in our own development. There is no sense in getting better and better at what you're already very good at.
- **Social cue adeptness.** The ability to understand from your observation and listening what is appropriate behavior or an appropriate response in widely divergent environments and circumstances.
- **Judgment.** The ability to discern between fighting for a principle and surrendering cordially to a matter of taste, and acting appropriately on all occasions.

You may choose to add to my list or alter it, but I've found these factors to be the bedrock, the underlying traits, of wise people. They lead to trust in your own judgment, *and the key difference between people of high and low self-esteem is the ability to trust in, and take action based on, their own judgment.* You can "buy" certain expertise and talents, but you can't buy judgment.

Faith in your own judgment is one of the key conditions that sets wise people apart. I call that trust the "critical gyroscope," because it keeps us balanced and upright, and enables us to maintain our equanimity despite what goes on around us.

That trust in your judgment, based on the hyper-traits I've outlined, leads to effective decision-making and behaviors, the navigation that directs your life and keeps you on course. More often than not, the result is success; and by "success," I mean meeting the criteria for your defined future, not the arbitrary metrics assigned by anyone else.

Sometimes, of course, we encounter a setback, and success is not immediate. This is where resilience is required, *and we tend to have the proper resilience when those hyper-traits are present.* They are a contingent reserve that serves us not only in improving our trust in our judgment but also in rebounding from loss or setback. That application drives us back to ultimate success.

This sequence is what I've derived from having observed and worked with tens of thousands of people over three decades in organizations, non-profits, athletics, entertainment, and educational institutions all over the globe. Intellectual health is a function of the ability to crisply bring your critical thinking skills to the pivotal issues. Once the process I've described is institutionalized—becomes unconscious competency—you can do this naturally and quite impressively.

This ability makes you far more valuable and is not age related, except for the fact that we tend to expect it more from a person of maturity. (When we see this behavior in a younger person, we tend to think "prodigy" or "savant" to explain the distinct exception.)

"Eliminating Scarcity in Your Soul," my title for this chapter, refers to the abstract worries that something isn't right, that something is somehow missing. I've found that what's missing is the confidence that comes from being physically, emotionally, psychologically, and intellectually sound. We can proactively and continually address these areas in a pragmatic manner. By so doing, we raise our self-worth and consequent willingness to express ourselves and impress ourselves upon the world around us.

Threescore and more can easily entail "full health" under the circumstances, if that's your philosophy, intent, and investment. We don't automatically lose acuity as we age unless we believe it's inevitable.

I'm telling you it's anything but.

Notables

Melchora Aquino de Ramos, 84. Became a hero of the Philippine Revolution against Spain.

Tony Randall, 75. Fathered his first child with his 50-years-younger second wife (and fathered another 2 years later).

Alexander Fleming, 64. Received the Nobel Prize in Physiology or Medicine for discovering penicillin.

Oscar Swahn, 72. Competed in the Olympics, the oldest sportsman to do so; won an Olympic gold medal at age 64 and remains the oldest gold medalist of the Olympics.

Carl Reiner, 95. Comedian, director, writer, producer, winner of nine Emmy Awards and a Grammy Award.

Angela Lansbury, 91. Award-winning actor on stage, screen, and television, as well as producer, singer, and songwriter.

Clint Eastwood, 87. Actor, producer, director, antiwar activist, politician; net worth over $375 million.

Barbara Walters, 86. Reporter and interviewer for ABC; when 75, was voted one of the 50 greatest TV stars of all time.

Notes

1. "Life Expectancy for Countries," infoplease, 2017, https://www.infoplease.com/world/health-and-social-statistics/life-expectancy-countries-0.
2. It was a behavioral consulting firm using such psychometric testing from which I was fired long ago. I recognized quite quickly how weak and misleading many of the results were and the ensuing dangers for careers.
3. Gregg Henriques, "What Constitutes Psychological Health?" *Psychology Today*, April 3, 2015, https://www.psychologytoday.com/blog/theory-knowledge/201504/what-constitutes-psychological-health.

CHAPTER 9

Healthy Outrage

We are often enslaved to people because we hold a grudge over a perceived slight. Yet that person is unaware, so they can't "free" us, and we remain trapped. There are healthy techniques to choose your fights, vent pressure, and salve your ego. Most of all, there is tolerance and forgiveness, which come with maturity and lead you to understand that the idiot who didn't use the signal when turning in front of you was not out to get you.

How to Vent

We need to relieve pressure in healthy ways using safe outlets. Pressure gauges on machinery indicate when dangerous levels are reached so that we can prevent problems—explosions. Some machinery is self-regulating and can shut down automatically. Humans aren't like that.

And our "pressure" is blood pressure, and that's a real issue as we age. So it's best to keep it under control.

We can't prevent pressures, but we can mitigate them. First, let's keep things in perspective. For example, a longer lifespan *does not mean* quantity without quality. Additional years of life are predominantly healthy ones. Five of the additional years a British boy born in 2015 can expect to live, compared with one born as recently as 1990, will be healthy.[1] We are no longer in a position where traditional retirement age is an unknown void full of incapacity and death.

Life stages are social constructs. What we call them and how we treat them is within our control and informs our behaviors. We could easily change the nomenclature from "elderly" to "gerontocracy," for example.

Understand, also, the economic power of the mature. In Western Europe, people over 60 will constitute almost 60 percent of consumption growth between now and 2030, according to McKinsey & Company.[2] We alluded earlier to the pragmatic need for the Japanese to have an older sales force to properly sell and service high net worth, older customers.

Perspective is important in healthy venting because we need understanding and not frustration. There are issues that are important and need to be corrected or otherwise addressed, and there are issues that are unimportant and merely need to be tolerated.

Venting when we stub a toe or twist an ankle is fine. Shouting expletives alone in your garage when you spill paint is understandable. But shouting obscenities when you hear bad news on the phone in an airline business club (as often happens) is not. Venting about something you can no longer do—such as play touch football or hike 20 miles—is all right if you are expressing a mild regret, but not if it's an ulcer-inducing tirade. Expressing grief is important, but treating every setback as a grief experience is silly—and immature.

When we are engaged in activities that have high meaning for us—and recall that we discussed *creating* meaning for yourself, not searching for it or using someone else's metric for meaning—and they create happiness, we are in a constant success state.

When the activities are meaningful—for example, a job or a volunteer position—but make us unhappy, we are sacrificing in order to complete the task. This may be useful or even necessary for a brief time—such as when you agree to raise funds for a good cause, even though you hate asking people for money—but on a long-term basis it's simply martyrdom. That creates great stress.

When we are very happy with an activity of low meaning—video games, sports shows, drugs—our lives range from stimulating to addictive. We're happy, perhaps, but not contributing and not engaged with others, except those who share in our stimulating but low-meaning activities. *A great many "retirees" simply sit home and watch sports reruns or do crossword puzzles.*

Finally, when happiness and meaning are both low, we are merely surviving, arising each day to wander through life, barely sentient.

Our need to vent will be less if we are in the upper-right quadrant of Figure 9.1. That's not only because we're in a success state but also because we'll be of a mindset to more readily deal with setbacks and challenges. Our judgment and perspective will be better (see "Intellectual Health" in the previous chapter).

But when we're sacrificing, we feel more pressure and more need to vent.

- I hate this, but no one else will do it.
- I'm not cut out for this.
- This won't get done unless I do it myself.
- How did I get into this and how do I get out of it?

Figure 9.1 *Happiness and meaning.*

When we're merely stimulated, we can also experience more pressure and a greater need to vent.

- I never have enough time to enjoy myself.
- Why can't I get better at this game?
- Why do they keep interrupting me when I'm busy?
- I wish I could do more of this somehow.

My point here is this: Concentrate on moving toward high-meaning and high-happiness pursuits, both in work and life. Vent about appropriate issues, such as someone's failure to meet a deadline, a poor-quality product, or a lousy experience, but not about "growing old" or things you think you can no longer do. If you find yourself venting excessively, and doing so inappropriately—in public, loudly, with obscenity—then ask yourself if you need to move from the sacrificing quadrant or the addictive quadrant.

When your pressure gauge (blood pressure) is getting too high due to stress around you,

- Talk to your spouse, your partner, a friend, or a colleague.
- Apply your perspective and judgment: How bad is this in the grand scheme of things?
- Ask yourself if you are you engaged in too much sacrifice.
- Consider whether you are addicted to a pursuit in an unhealthy manner.
- Try to vent privately for a brief period in a healthy way.
- Think of ways that you can remove the stress or mitigate its effects.
- If your stress is a one-time event, deal with it; if it's recurrent or ongoing, eliminate it entirely.
- Find a counselor, coach, or clergy member who is sensitive to the issues you are experiencing to advise you.

Ego Restraint

A second aspect of what I call "healthy outrage" is ego restraint. That doesn't mean being egoless or humble. Here's famed architect Frank Lloyd Wright on humility: "Early in life I had to choose between honest arrogance and hypocritical humility. I chose honest arrogance and have seen no occasion to change."

If you journey through life with your ego on the bow of the ship, it's going to be battered and bruised by the winds and waves. There is no reason for it to be there. Tuck it away.

However, as we age we tend to grow somewhat sensitive and fall into the trap of seeking victimization. This is one of the great failures in modern society: claiming that you're not more successful because "they" won't allow you to be. I saw a woman in a wheelchair at an event maneuver into a line for refreshments much too close to the man in front of her. When he inevitably turned and bumped into her, she said, "Oh, sure, just ignore me down here!" She was a professional victim.

But so are people who claim that they are discriminated against because of their age when, in fact, they are not. That's not to say there is no age discrimination; I've tried to establish at the outset that there is. But I've also tried to establish how you can overcome it through the retention and building of power and control. *In over 30 years of consulting, I've never seen an organization with rational leadership that deliberately terminated people with talent who could significantly help the organization.* Irrational leadership is the exception, not the rule (e.g., "Chainsaw Al Dunlap" at Scott Paper, whose "turnaround" efforts were actually fraudulent).

I was once asked to coach a woman who told me she had been let go from three previous jobs in succession over 5 years because of her age and "politics" (she was in her early sixties). I told her the odds of three such successive terminations due to politics or age were not likely (after all, she was hired at roughly the same age at which she was terminated). I quickly realized she was a poor performer and a professional victim. Her age was irrelevant; her attitude was the issue.

Ego restraint means the correct application of ego (which is your sense of self-worth). Carl Reiner, one of my "Notables" and a producer, director, writer, and comedian who is active at 95, speaking "as a nonagenarian who has just completed the most prolific, productive five years of my life," urged Supreme Court Justice Anthony Kennedy not to retire at a mere 81.[3]

Humility is often seen as the opposite of the dreaded "arrogance," yet we seem to have a distorted sense of what arrogance is. Let me give you a brief test.

There are two consultants, both with excellent credentials. One doesn't believe in self-promotion and relies on the good graces of client referrals to continue to gain business. The other believes in aggressive self-promotion in order to provide value to more clients.

Who is more arrogant?

The answer is the first consultant, who believes he is so good that the world will come to him, and he can sit by the phone without making any further effort. The second, however, is far more humble, believing she has great value to offer and it's therefore incumbent upon her to reach out to prospects so they can explore her help for them.

Hiding your abilities is never a good idea in organizations, and that's especially true as you age. The more apparent and impressive your judgment and wisdom are, the more invaluable you become. If you review my Notables lists, from Carl Reiner to Tom Brady to Tony Bennett or any of the others, their careers aren't going to end despite their talents because they've reached a certain age. Their careers continue *because of their talents and because they're so visible.*

It's our job, in all humility, to continue to make our talents and results highly visible. To expect someone else to do that for us is the height of arrogance.

Ego restraint also allows us to avoid taking offense at the slightest issue. I believe that unnecessary exception and accommodation are inadvertent attempts to deprive people of power and control. We should avoid them when they are not needed. *But we needn't be offended at the offer.* If someone offers a senior discount or asks if we'd like to board the plane early, such proffers are not meant to be insulting and shouldn't be seen as such.

Of course, when someone says, "You're too old" for a job that has no age sensitivity, or "We need someone younger" when youth is irrelevant, it is time to take offense and express healthy outrage. The trick is having the discretion to know when offense is deliberate (or the result of bias) and when it is inadvertent.

One of the saddest things I see as a frequent traveler is a parade of people who take advantage of early boarding on an aircraft when there isn't anything obviously wrong with them, though they tend to be older people. I don't argue that they might have heart conditions or breathing problems. But most of these people are the first ones off the plane, rushing up a jetway similar to one they labored down at the beginning of the journey. This is demeaning to all of us, because it's taking advantage and not retaining power.

Manipulation isn't power. Gaming the system isn't control.

We'll deal in detail in the next segments about how to react to offense, intended or unintended, and what to ignore and what to combat. But for now, ask yourself:

- Do you need the special seating on public vehicles or in airport waiting areas?
- Do you need special treatment or discounts?
- If you're not physically incapacitated, do you still expect privileges others don't have?

In your organizational life:

- Are you vocal and assertive, or do you expect others will automatically ask your advice?
- Do you assume that you'll be seen as an elder statesman or do you realize that you must impress your views on others with logic and pragmatism?

- Do you exhibit the energy (not physical strength) to lead teams, champion a cause, resist bad ideas?

The woman who told me she was disabled because she was over 65 and could therefore park (illegally) wherever she wanted was extraordinarily depressing. She believed (or at least wanted others to believe) that merely gaining certain birthdays was incapacitating. She thought that would give her a societal advantage of a very small sort.

But, in fact, it created an ostracism and separatism that was not otherwise justified. She thought she was playing the system, but she was actually removing herself from it.

Tolerance

Ironically, one of the most important aspects of healthy outrage is the discretion to know when to apply it and when not to. The opposite of healthy outrage is tolerance.

Tolerance, too, can be dysfunctional when excessive. We should never tolerate a degree of poor service in a restaurant that results in cold food, or in an airline that results in lost luggage, or in a doctor that results in an hour's wait at every appointment. But we can tolerate an error in recording a phone number, or the wrong morning newspaper, or the wrong size coffee at the café.

Maturity allows for a "larger picture" perspective. If we are constantly outraged, we're constantly stressed. I was always befuddled by clients who poured on the stress during the day, then provided an on-site gym to work it off at lunch or after work! It might have been better to reduce the stress levels to begin with.

On an individual level, we can control stress by calibrating when outrage is appropriate (a biased comment about aging) and when tolerance is appropriate (a comment that you aren't using the latest technology). *There is a reverse ageism, which consists of being critical of all things not of our generation.*

Personally, I don't care for a great deal of modern music. I think it ranges from nonmelodic to degrading (especially of women). I grew up as the last of an era when parents and children—two generations—were listening to the same music: the post–World War II "great American songbook," moving from the big band era to star singers as embodied by Frank Sinatra.

In the 50s, Dick Clark and *American Bandstand* came along, and Elvis ushered in rock 'n' roll as the "new Sinatra," and the elder generation condemned the new music. A rift began that seems to continue generationally. The Beatles, briefly (I think), once gain combined the musical tastes of disparate people, but they were alone in so doing.

Comedy is similar. Everyone once listened to Bob Hope and Jack Benny, and later Johnny Carson was a great unifier on *The Tonight Show*. But with few exceptions today (Jerry Seinfeld?) comedy, too, is generational. I have no interest in listening to "comedy" that is merely a succession of profanity every five words. To me, that's the worst kind of anti-intellectualism.

But I tolerate others' tastes so long as they don't undermine the quality of my life. I don't have to watch the comedy cable channels I find revolting, and I can choose my music in my home or car or headset. If you want to mock me for not using Instagram, that's your prerogative, I have no use for it. And I find Facebook a huge vanity press and time dump. On the other hand, Twitter is an excellent retail marketing tool, which I use mightily to promote my books.

You don't have to embrace others' lifestyles, but you can't arbitrarily reject them. We can't afford to isolate ourselves from the diversity around us. It's as appalling for people to eschew someone above a certain age on a committee or project as it is to decline to include people below a certain age. We have some excellent politicians in their twenties and thirties, and some horrible ones in their fifties, sixties, and above. Age does not automatically bestow wisdom. As I've noted, wisdom requires work that is enhanced with age.

Reverse ageism—rejecting art, effort, opinions, or creations merely because of the age of those behind them—is offensive. It demonstrates a lack of tolerance and an unwillingness to even attempt acceptance. When you roll your eyes and think, "Here we go again," every time a young person suggests something different from your belief system (or tastes) at that moment, you're not really hiding your antipathy. And you're shutting yourself out of the dynamic.

Tolerance is a result of the judgment we discussed earlier, knowing when a principle needs defending and when taste justifies a compromise or concession. It's an important consideration in all aspects of our lives. Most major religions speak in some way of the virtues of tolerance and forgiveness (the latter we'll discuss next). But you don't need to be a religious person to understand the salutary benefits of being tolerant, especially in these areas:

- **Family.** Most of us have a cousin Eddy or an Aunt Betty who can rile us easily. We know it's coming at a family event or holiday dinner when someone gets drunk, or criticizes the meal, or wonders why you don't do more for them. This type of fighting is a Sisyphean endeavor. It will never be resolved. How much of your lifetime do you want to spend combatting it? It's far better to tolerate the barbs and behavior without encouraging more.

- **Generations.** It's pretty hopeless to try to make your kids poor. That is, you can't replicate the experiences that molded you and made you who you are. Nor should you. But you can imbue values. (We're often better with grandchildren because we don't have to live with them 24 hours a day!) We need to be tolerant of contemporary habits and preferences (video games, constant texting) but draw the line at clear dangers (drinking while driving, experimenting with drugs).

- **Employment.** Constant battles with co-workers undermine everyone's productivity, including our own. Continually blaming the boss for every inconvenience and problem is a fool's errand. If you have to be someplace every day, then it only makes sense to tolerate those around you who may have differing ideas and approaches without constant argument and strife. The other option, if they are *in*tolerable, is to leave. But if you can't tolerate most people around you, the chances are it's your issue, not theirs.

- **Entrepreneurialism.** We have to tolerate those who always have a better idea, insist our ideas won't work, or refuse to support us. Being creative means being willing to stand apart and not need validation from others. However, it also means being tolerant of others. I've experienced people trying to sell me something or convince me to support them who were outraged (and not healthily) when I declined. There were zealots who were unfulfilled until they achieved a convert. We must tolerate those who don't agree with our new direction or ideas, not simply dismiss them or, worse, attack them.

- **Politics and polity.** When I visited the Acropolis in Athens, I learned that the word accounts for "high" (hence, "acrophobia," a fear of heights) and "public" (hence, "police" and "politics"). Our lack of tolerance for dissenting opinions today has created huge polarization in our society and has stifled honest debate, has led to the shouting down of guest speakers, and has prompted the labeling of those opposing our point of view with epithets and negative descriptors, effectively preventing any attempt at understanding opposing views. This is a far cry from "the high place." We need to be tolerant most of all in our social and political dealings, or we run the risk of isolating ourselves and even contributing to the biases inherent in ageism.

Healthy outrage is counterbalanced by two strong forces of power and control: tolerance and forgiveness.

Forgiveness

As some of you no doubt recognize, Christ, especially, talked about tolerance and forgiveness, fundamental tenets of Christianity. By no means am

I attempting to sneak religion into this book, other than to point out the obvious: We all, at our best, require forgiveness for ourselves and should bestow it on others who require it.

The final necessity of healthy outrage is to get over it. That's sometimes a logical process, sometimes subject to coaching, sometimes requiring therapy, and too often seen as impossible. We marvel at people who openly forgive someone who has killed a relative, those who have opposed the killer's death sentence. It may seem that they are going overboard to calm a third party who delivered trauma to them.

But it is more probable they are providing calm for themselves.

Forgiveness is an act of kindness for yourself. It is effective when venting, ego restraint, and tolerance haven't worked sufficiently well (or at all). We often hold onto grudges and resentment and umbrage. Yet, often enough, the other person doesn't realize it. They don't understand that they've hurt us in some way (and, perhaps, they haven't and we just imagined it).

Consequently, we have become enslaved to people we cannot forgive for their actions but who don't have the capacity to free us since they don't understand they've hurt us in reality or perceptually.

That's why forgiveness is the only remedy. We can forgive in person and based on a real event: "You hurt me yesterday when you told me to shut up because my points weren't valid. I understand you felt pressured and threatened, and I forgive you for those comments. But please never do that again." We can forgive in our minds based on our perceptions: "I don't believe she meant to hurt me when she neglected to open my gift, and I'm sure if she realized what had happened, she would have apologized."

These are acts of closure. They are vitally important as we age.

Time provides the unfortunate opportunity to accrete grievances and perceived slights. If we don't provide forgiveness, these slights collect like weeds in a garden and eventually crowd out all other plants' ability to take root and find nourishment. Where once there were flowers and brightness, there is now only chaos and blandness.

When we fill our lives with unforgiven events and treatment, we create horrible dynamics:

- We stop dealing with people who can help us.
- We exclude people who could be important in our lives.
- We automatically disregard advice from expert parties.
- We build our stress levels when we recall the "transgressions."
- We infect others around us, especially children: "Don't befriend people like this."
- We create emotional shields to protect us from *all others*.
- We try to retaliate.

I think you can see the illnesses and dysfunctions building up, and I think you can recognize them in your own behaviors. As kids, we "hated" other kids and wouldn't forgive them—until the next football game or party. Sometimes we carried the grievance onward, but we tended to outgrow it. One sign of emotional instability is taking umbrage at some petty problem from 10 years or more ago—for example, someone at a class reunion still taking offense at a long-ago slight.

The "secret" of long-term marriages and relationships is forgiveness. You have a spat over lunch and enjoy a swim in the afternoon.

However, the adherence of grudges grows from that of a sticky note to superglue strength as we age, if we're not careful. We eternally blame a boss for a job we didn't get (a promotion over which the boss may or may not have actually had influence). We retain bitterness over an offhand comment about our hair, accessories, outfit, or vacation choice. We regret not having been more forceful in defending ourselves at the time, and consequently become "enslaved" to the individual who offended us, wittingly or unwittingly, advertently or inadvertently.

If we're not careful, by the time threescore comes around, we have a Wikipedia of entries for people who have somehow earned our enmity at work, within our extended family, in the community, and among other professionals in our field.

Digression

One type of person most difficult for anyone to deal with is the classic passive-aggressive. This is the person who avoids direct conflict by using indirect and subtle taunts, critique, and demeaning attitudes.

An example was a woman whose children graduated high school with ours, whom I'll call "Molly." Molly would damn with faint praise. If your child was admitted into the University of Michigan, for example, she'd say, "Congratulations, I assume that was her backup school?" Or "That's a wonderful outfit, and I'm sure it was stunning when you first bought it." Or "Your husband went to college? I would have never known."

The way to deal with passive-aggressive behavior is to confront it: "Why would you say such a deliberately hurtful thing? You knew exactly how that would be received—as disrespectful." It's only when we don't confront it that we feel mistreated afterward, and we create everlasting unhappiness for ourselves and antipathy directed at the other person.

Deal with the behavior at the time or forgive it after the fact. These people suffer from an emotional illness and will not change.

How do we best forgive? Forgiveness does take a great deal of personal confidence and intention. But we all do it. Here are best practices:

- We *do* forgive people every day. Why? We realize an innocent error or even a bad goof can be overcome. The coffee didn't have sweetener in it; the shop forgot to pack one of our purchases. These things happen.
- We forgive because we cause further damage by not forgiving. Should we berate the poor airline clerk who didn't personally lose our luggage but is resentful of our tone and demands, or should we simply ask

what we can do to better help the clerk locate our luggage, since blame is useless when recovery is the point?

- When were we most thankful to be forgiven? When we forgot a dinner engagement or didn't remember a birthday or ruined a vacation by packing the wrong gear? What were our reactions on occasions when others berated us constantly or when others said, "Don't worry, I've done the same thing. Let's make the best of it."

- Free yourself from the demons, the stress, the unfulfilled need. Cut the cord to the weight you're dragging around. Do you really want to waste time, as your horizon grows closer, being mentally and emotionally upset about events that can't be undone and people who can't "free" you anyway?

- Understand that death is a terminal, not a station. In other words, not forgiving someone who can no longer be held to account, interact with you, or otherwise make you feel better is unstable. It is an emotional liability that you must release for your own health.

"Forgive and forget" seems like advice so simple that it's useless. But in reality, it's the final anodyne for using and moving on from healthy outrage. And it will help you defy age by ridding you of the encumbrances that build up often unknowingly and unrecognized over time.

Notables

Gene Fastook, at this writing, is 92. He is a captain in the police auxiliary in New York City. He works in the 47th Precinct station house. He checks the duty roster and oversees who will be checking in so that all positions are staffed properly. He prides himself on saving money for the police department and the taxpayers.

Mr. Fastook served in World War II and Korea, was present when MacArthur walked onto the beach on his return to the Philippines, inspected material for the space program, met Wernher von Braun, and was known by John Glenn.

Oh, yes: He's only the second-oldest person in the New York City Police Department.[4]

Notes

1. Institute for Health Metrics and Evaluation, University of Washington, cited in "What to Call the Time of Life between Work and Old Age," *Economist*, July 8, 2017.
2. Ibid.
3. Carl Reiner, "Justice Kennedy, Take It from Me: Never Retire," *New York Times*, July 10, 2017, Sunday Review.
4. Jim Dwyer, "He Helped Reach Moon; His Encore: The Bronx," *New York Times*, July 19, 2017.

CHAPTER 10

Defying Age

Pain is unavoidable in aging, but suffering is voluntary. Our losses may be familial, collegial, or even related to abilities, but they can be overcome and used as strengths. Our relationships to the world around us and to others are the crucial elements in sustaining and improving our strengths while accommodating our losses. Why are we opposed to suicide yet so often sacrifice life piecemeal on a daily basis?

Dealing with Inevitable Loss

I once scoffed at the idea of holding wakes and sitting shiva. The latter is a week-long mourning in the Jewish faith, the former is a watch over the body that once lasted several days but is now more commonly a single day for some Christians. Years ago, it wasn't unusual for professional mourners to be hired to add wailing and drama to these rites.

As I matured I came to realize that the rituals weren't an unwillingness to let go of a loved one but rather a release point. The mourning was defined, circumscribed, and brief. We were permitted to release our sadness, acknowledge the dead, extend our sympathies—and move on.

As we age, loss in all forms multiplies. Thus, it's more important than ever to understand it, expect it, and deal with it successfully. Denial cannot be an aspect of it. To this day, many Japanese people, in collusion with doctors, will not tell a family member who has the disease that they have a deadly form of cancer. They use euphemisms and sometimes outright lies to try to ease the pain. And we often lie to each other about the severity of an impeding loss or its inevitability.

I've met people who are devastated over the loss of a pet, which is quite understandable. But then they are almost unable to function for extended periods, personally and professionally, which is not understandable. Such losses are inevitable—dogs, for example, depending on breed, tend to live about 10 to 15 years—and we should neither deny that fact nor unreasonably extend the mourning (or expect immortality).

When we are exceptionally close to someone, such as a spouse, a partner, or a parent who lives with us, the loss can feel unbearable. But if losses were unbearable, none of us would be here today. I wouldn't be writing this and you wouldn't be reading it. Life goes on.

In the worst of times, we have to realize that "this, too, shall pass."

So let me be clear: I am not denying that loss is real; I am telling you that it is inevitable and must be dealt with successfully. By "successfully," I mean that your emotions deserve an outlet, and your life will be somewhat altered, but that your life also goes on, your contributions continue, and your loss can add to your growth. And I am telling you that as we age we must become adept at this because loss is more frequent.

I've chosen to start with the most serious kind of loss: families, friends, partnerships, colleagues—human loss. Even revered figures we've never met can generate huge feelings of loss; people lined the streets in tears when Franklin Roosevelt and John F. Kennedy died. People lie in state when they are beloved public figures in the arts, sports, religion, politics, and humanitarianism, for example.

But a wide variety of other losses will occur. Let's first take a look at losses beyond other people, and then examine what to do about loss.

- **Pets.** We anthropomorphize our pets so that they are far more than merely animals. They are sources of unconditional love, amusement, camaraderie, and friendship. Whether it's a cat, bird, or fish, the pet provides us with companionship that is uncomplaining, nonjudgmental, and important in our lives.

- **Surroundings.** It's difficult to leave a home or a place that has provided comfort and fond memories. Sometimes we have to downsize our living arrangements, often because children leave home. Sometimes we have to move for work, or relationships, or health. We experience restaurants, clubs, and gathering places that disappear through others' departure or development, or simply because of lack of support.

- **Abilities.** We will be hampered by inevitabilities associated with aging, such as arthritis, joint problems, stamina issues, and disease and sickness. Yet these are not nearly as fatal as they once were.[1] (We discussed earlier that mental decline is not an automatic aspect of aging.)

- **Interests and pursuits.** No matter the level of our physical conditioning, we may not be able to scuba dive or kickbox or alpine ski. That doesn't apply to all of us, perhaps, but there are certain physical limitations on some pursuits, despite the fact that our own health may be just fine.

So how do we prepare ourselves for these eventualities? How do we prevent an ongoing grief magnified by the accumulation of losses?

1. **Create offsetting gains.** When someone loses a pet, my advice (and we've always had pets) is to immediately obtain a new one. The spirit of the other animal will live in the new one. If you're replacing a dog, try to acquire a rescue animal that could use a good home.

   I'm not suggesting you go out and find a new spouse (immediately)! But we need to have so many diverse relationships that one loss can be overcome through the continued strengths of other important relationships. This is why we discussed earlier the importance of friends and colleagues of diverse ages and backgrounds. We went to an inordinate number of weddings after college graduation because we were all the same age, but we don't want our current friends to be all the same age so that everyone departs at once! We must have ongoing means of replacing loss, not in a physical one-for-one sense, but rather in the dynamics of the meaningful relationships that were created and are so important to us.

2. **Give yourself the right to mourn, but in two phases.** Phase one is your immediate grief. Take a few days. Remember what was so valuable. Plan for the proper respect and acknowledgment, such as a gathering of friends. Phase two is your ongoing remembrance. A man down the road lost his young dog and planted a tree with a plaque to remind him of the dog daily. The tree is now several years old and 12 feet high, and prompts us to remember him too. Giving yourself permission for ongoing remembrance is an important recovery aspect, whether it's a yearly anniversary, a photo on the wall, or occasional time for some memories.

3. **Find new meaning.** A new job, new home, new club, or new surroundings all have huge potential to contribute to your happiness and success. What you had in the past was hugely important but seldom singular. It's up to you to create and sustain new meaning, by making your surroundings comfortable and supportive, becoming a "regular," developing new friends, creating new hobbies.

4. **Pursue new interests.** You may not be able to scuba dive, but you can probably snorkel. Kickboxing may be out, but yoga may be in. If you can't ride a motorcycle, what about a bike? If you look through my "Notables" at the end of each chapter, you'll find people who started new pursuits late in life and with great success.

These are methods to get over the pain. But what about the suffering?

The Difference between Pain and Suffering

The martyrs love the work.

Pain is physical and/or mental hurt caused by illness, disease, or distress. The physical and mental aspects of pain can be separate or may accompany each other. One often leads to the other, as a long illness can cause mental anguish, and high stress levels are connected with high blood pressure, stroke, and other physical ailments.

To suffer is to be subjected, voluntarily or involuntarily, to unpleasantness. We may suffer through a boring speech we can't escape, a loss described in the previous segment, or a poor golf round.

Pain is usually out of our control and unavoidable, though there are exceptions, such as carelessly stepping where you shouldn't. Suffering is usually within our control, though there are exceptions, such as being forced to be in the presence of a horrid individual.

A vast difference in people's ability and effectiveness as they age is in the way they react to pain and suffering. We can endure pain and nevertheless have a positive attitude because we've chosen not to suffer. People with diseases, illnesses, stark disadvantages, and surprising setbacks have chosen not to suffer, despite the pain. Yet others, with minor afflictions and even perceived slights, choose to suffer continually.

If you don't believe me, just read Facebook.

I tire of people—and no one wants to hire or help or trust people—who believe they are suffering through life. There is no law or rule that says the world has to accommodate your every petty grievance or whim, or that no one else can go about their business until you are completely happy—which will never occur, in any case.

Here are examples of people choosing to suffer—often subconsciously—in their daily lives. Think about whether any of this pertains to you.

- Grief and complaints over traffic jams that make you late (often for an appointment you've allowed too little time to reach). This often includes irrational rants, such as hoping it's a serious accident and not a mere fender-bender to at least "justify" the delay!
- Obsession over the loss of a loved one for months (and even years), to the point of being unable to function well, requiring constant commiseration and becoming depressed. I heard one person consider giving up his work because a pet had died, expectedly, at an advanced age.

- Blame laid on the boss (or co-workers or subordinates) daily for a perceived inability to get things done yourself. This becomes a mantra and closes off all introspection and self-analysis.
- Hypochondria that turns every cough, mole, and pain into reasons not to do things, visits to the doctor, and even denial of proof that there's nothing wrong.
- An unwillingness to do something at all just because you can't do it as well as you once did. Some bursitis prevents you from skiing as fast as you used to on black diamond hills, so you give up the sport entirely, even though you're still better than most and enjoy the outdoors.
- Suffering after the actual pain has departed. Harking back to an incident and lamenting that you could have done more or enjoyed yourself more if only you weren't indisposed or if only you were your "normal self." This is a form of sustained suffering that many of us never surrender.
- A refusal to remove the cause of or walk away from the acknowledged pain. These include avoiding "unthinkable" acts such as changing your job, ending a relationship, delegating some work, refusing to attend, and so forth. To take these mature and corrective steps would disable the excuse for the suffering and its expression. And that is why you can't pity the martyrs, because they love the work and won't leave it.

Digression

I was facilitating a session at the American Press Institute among a group of star reporters. They all complained about their work at one time or another, but one guy, from the *New York Times*, was vociferous. I asked him for examples.

He said, "They [management] don't respect us. We're not paid well, our equipment is old, the hours are ridiculous. Some of our best work is ignored. It's a daily battle."

"Why don't you leave the profession?" I asked.

"Are you crazy?" he yelled. "I love this work!"

If you think about professions that attract those with a passion for the job—journalism, nursing, teaching, police work, firefighting, medical rescue work—they aren't highly paid. That's not because they aren't of great value—they are some of the most valuable roles in our society—but rather because the people who pursue these careers love the work. They put up with the minor pains but engage in major suffering, which actually detracts from their performance. (Just ask a cop someday what he or she thinks of their superiors, or a nurse of the doctors.)

So what's the lesson for us?

We will, inevitably, face pain, whether physical or emotional. We all know there are conditions that will exacerbate that probability, such as having kids, pets, parents living within our homes, and so forth. The question becomes this: To what degree are we willing and able to try to minimize and even eliminate the suffering that might otherwise accompany it?

Your child messing up in school can be painful, but constantly asking yourself, "Where did I go wrong?" is unhelpful and unproductive.

I think at this point you can see the relationship between suffering and guilt (which we discussed in Chapter 7). Guilt causes suffering, and suffering causes and extends guilt. We have to escape that particular doom loop. Guilt is a catalyst for suffering, and the longer we engage in it—which is more deadly over a long lifetime—the more we endanger our health and our ability to perform.

One of the most important elements of continued success at threescore and more is to avoid this doom loop or to escape from it by

- Eliminating guilt
- Acknowledging appropriate pain and reducing it

- Confining suffering to as brief a period as possible
- Removing yourself from situations causing suffering
- Refusing martyrdom

Spirituality

This is a topic that scares a great many people, and perhaps you're among them. I saved it until the penultimate segment for that reason (and the ultimate segment sometimes scares people even more). It scares people because it immediately connotes "dreaded" religion to many and to others a sort of *woo-woo* approach to rapping tables and contact with lost souls.[2]

Assuming you haven't dropped the book and run into traffic, let me define spirituality so that we can deal with my point rationally: Spirituality is a connection with nature and the world around you. A spiritual person is one who sees meaning and value in the surrounding world and immediate environment. To be spiritual is to be integrated with and an interacting part of the world around you.

Spiritual people see optimism, opportunity, and opulence around them. They are, by default, positive and effervescent. They see no shame in laughing or crying as the condition warrants. They are vulnerable and open, candid and honest.

I doubt that all religious people (even members of the clergy) are spiritual, and I believe atheists are often spiritual. This is not a religious calling or tenet, nor a belief in or denial of God. It does not mean spirit as in "ghosts" or alcohol, but is closer to the intent of the observation "She's a spirited person" or "He's always in high spirits."

I raise this issue under "defying age" because I know of no better means to be forever vibrant and alive. "Forever young" is a metaphor; forever exciting or fascinating or attractive is, however, an observation.

Digression

Azriel Blackman is a mechanic with American Airlines who joined the company at 16 and worked on the famous "flying boats" that were the first transoceanic service. He's being feted now, at 92, as the longest-serving airline employee at American or anywhere, as attested by the ubiquitous Guinness people.

He still works a 5:00 a.m. to 1:00 p.m. day, 5 days a week, as a shift supervisor. He can't drive out on the tarmac anymore, nor handle a wrench, but he can supervise and process paperwork. Robert L. Crandall, CEO of American, says that Mr. Blackman represents a vital institutional memory, a commitment to quality, and a valuable transmission to younger employees (in other words, all other employees).

Mr. Blackman has no plans to retire.[3]

Why does it help to be spiritual, especially as we age?
It helps for these reasons:

- The world around us is confusing and ambiguous. We're not really sure we're alone in the universe, nor what the universe is. There are constant threats of disease, war, terror, natural disaster, accident, and turmoil. It's easy to feel we have no control, as we've examined earlier.

   Being connected provides a feeling of control. We appreciate and interact with the world around us. We don't rely on what others say, on social media, or on rumors. We see for ourselves. If we solely heeded the threats that are publicized daily by viewer-seeking media sensationalism, we'd have good reason to never leave the house. Spiritual people know they have every reason to want to leave the house, because the world is a pretty wonderful place.

- As we age, our physical limitations can tend to make the world a smaller place. But our growing embrace of spirituality can prove it to be a highly expanding place. Appreciating the outdoors, respecting animals, exploring different seasons, and seeing beauty creates a growing perspective, and we've had time to do much more of those things than many others have. I've been with people who viewed a painting on a wall in a museum for an hour and came away with more understanding and happiness than someone who spent a week at Tahoe or St. Bart's.

- The interaction renews us. We are buoyed by dynamics that we partake of or even create. Walking on the beach at 7:00 a.m. before anyone else is about; sitting under a canopy of stars in the woods where there is no ambient light; watching bees industriously pollinate flowers in a garden; watching the dog catch a Frisbee, automatically calculating height, speed, and altitude and jumping at the precisely right moment, better than any $10 million center fielder.

- It brings calm. I've watched businesspeople look out the window at the cityscape for a few minutes before making a key decision. I've seen entertainers in the wings meditate before going on stage. I've seen athletes listen to their favorite music on earphones, alone, before the biggest contest of their careers.

Digression

I was watching a televised high school basketball game of the week, which featured top teams and professional announcers. The game was exciting and very close, with one player on one team carrying them down the stretch near the end of the game. But his team was down by two points and they needed to force overtime. He tried the last-second shot and missed but was fouled with no time left.

The tension was palpable and the announcers were beside themselves. As the player approached the foul line for his two shots, a teammate shouted encouragement—something like, "You can do it!" The star player turned to him and winked! The announcers went berserk, seeing this kind of cool in a high school kid.

He made both shots and they won in overtime.

Here are my suggestions for improving and increasing your spirituality as you age. If you feel you're already quite adept at this, then consider these recommendations for sustaining your skills. Remember that those who see conspiracies around us wherever they look are neither alert nor insightful; they are paranoid. Cynicism and paranoia are the opposites of spirituality. Nonspiritual people see a metaphorical "flat Earth," filled with threat and not promise, danger and not opportunity. You probably know or have known far too many of those people already.

1. Spend time looking around. Empty your mind. Take a few minutes to look at the house, the car, the neighborhood, your family, the pets, the neighbors. Ask yourself what you see. What are the connections? What makes sense and what doesn't? See my example of the Frisbee-catching dog, above. There's nothing "natural" about a dog catching a ball or, for that matter, a kid riding a bike.

2. Ask yourself "Why?" Why does the weather affect people the way it does? (There are more "meteorologists" on my local TV stations than there are reporters on the streets.) Why do some people react in some ways and others in diametrically opposite ways to the exact same stimuli? What do you see that is fascinating just because it exists, and why? (I've always marveled, when I stay in an upper floor in a New York City hotel, that there is architectural ornamentation on the tops of other buildings that cannot possibly be seen from the street. Why was it put there?)

3. Find connections. Bees pollinate because they need to make honey, not because they were ordered to help flowers reproduce. What other symbiosis is around you? Many (most?) people detest spiders and snakes,

yet both play an important ecological role. When people complained to John Muir, the legendary naturalist, about the problems with poison ivy and asked why it existed, Muir replied, "Maybe it was made for itself."

We often feel that life is obvious, as if we see it all, especially as we age. Nothing could be further from the truth. We have to constantly question it, examine it, and take part in it. That's spirituality.

Intimacy

An intimate relationship is an interpersonal dynamic that involves physical and/or emotional intimacy. Physical intimacy is characterized by friendship, platonic love, romantic love, or sexual activity. While the term intimate relationship commonly implies a sexual relationship, this obviously need not be so.

Such relationships play a critical role in the overall human experience. Humans have a general desire to belong and to love, which is usually satisfied within an intimate relationship. I believe this is more and more important as we age, to the point where intimacy can be pivotal, so I've chosen to end the discussion about "defying age" with this reality.

One of the most dire aspects of aging is loss. The longer we live, the more we lose. It's important to offset loss with gain. I know what you're thinking: Most losses can't be replaced, and we have fewer options that provide the gain.

I've tried to demonstrate in this book that the basic habits of retaining control, diversifying friends, and finding new pursuits removes us from the labels and stereotyping of "generational banalities." It's quite true that some losses are irreplaceable, but it's equally true that the temporary vacuum can be filled once again with fresh air.

Our losses include

- Family
- Friends
- Colleagues
- Homes
- Possessions
- Favorite visiting places
- Pets
- Hobbies
- Physical abilities

Yet we can gain in all of these areas. We can become closer to remaining family members, overcome petty disagreements, and make amends. We can develop new friends, colleagues, and hobbies. We can acquire new pets and take up activities commensurate with our physical capabilities. We can obtain new possessions, change homes, visit new places.

Loss does not have to be a one-sided, downward spiral if we choose not to allow it to be. But it's certainly not easy to replace and gain in all of these and other areas. (I've missed Palisades Park in Englewood, New Jersey, ever since they tore it down 50 years ago to build ugly apartments, but I've found other amusement venues to enjoy with my family. If we allow every one of these "losses" to degrade our lives we'll soon be unable to move from all that weight.)

The vital characteristic needed to deal with loss and create gains is intimacy.

Intimacy involves vulnerability. We have to admit to our grief, or longing, or loss, and allow others to help us. The first step in any healing process is to recognize the illness. We have to admit to our feelings and share them. At an Alcoholics Anonymous meeting, the first thing that people do when addressing the group is to state their first name and admit they are alcoholics. That strips away denial. Pretending that we don't have loss, that we don't miss things, that we're not worried about what's gone is denial and creates emotional barriers that preclude help.

Logic makes us think, emotions make us act. Engaging in intimacy is a step that allows our emotions to surface and guide us instead of remain hidden and undermine us.

Intimacy requires other people. You can't be intimate alone or with your dog. Ideally, we need people in our lives who can provide emotional, psychological, and physical intimacy. (It's documented that people engage in sexual activity well into their nineties, yet almost every study seems to be accompanied by underlying shock!) The "other people" need to be diverse, and not confined to our own generation. Throughout my career, I've coached and counseled people far older than I without anyone deciding that I was too young to do so. I accept advice today from people of all ages and backgrounds.

In addition to vulnerability, we must engage in reciprocity. One-way assistance, outside of medical care, seldom works. In fact, we learn more when we coach others than the people we coach, in most instances. The old admonition is accurate: If you want to learn something, try to teach it (or better, coach it). Counterintuitively, we gain intimacy when we give, not merely receive. We therein create mutual trust.

Commiseration is not what's needed to deal with loss. Nor do we need to hear that other people have coped with it well and here's their method. What we need is empathy, the sense that another understands our loss, which helps us through the pain and then shortens the suffering.

Finally, we need proportion. The loss of a parent, spouse, or child is indescribable. But the loss of a friend or colleague is less traumatic, and the loss of a home or vacation spot even less so. The loss of possessions is less upsetting still. Losing a pet is tough, but we know it will occur someday, and I've alluded earlier to the lack of proportion of people who lose a pet and think about closing their business or changing their lives. (These proportional considerations are by no means confined to aging but are more common the longer we live and so must be dealt with more frequently.)

Now is the time to consider and improve your intimate relationships and the components of vulnerability, reciprocity, and proportion. This is difficult to accomplish after a loss, especially after multiple losses. We need to create a life of intimacy now if we want to defy aging and its inevitable demands. It's never too late to begin this, but it does become more difficult.

My suggestions are these:

- Reestablish "broken links" among family, friends, and colleagues.
- Seek and acquire new friends and colleagues at diverse ages and points in their lives.
- Practice lowering emotional shields and share your concerns and insecurities with others.
- Offer and be receptive to others who want to share with you, to create reciprocity. (Don't think, "Oh, no, I'd really rather not hear about that divorce or hospital stay.")

- Maintain your perspective. Possessions, vacation sites, activities, hobbies, and so forth can all be replaced.

If you want to defy age, take it on boldly. It's not merely threescore, it's threescore and *more…*

Notes

1. For example, death rates due to cancer are down in the United States by 25 percent since 1991. Stacy Simon, "Cancer Facts and Figures," American Cancer Society, Jan 5, 2017, https://www.cancer.org/latest-news/cancer-facts-and-figures-death-rate-down-25-since-1991.html.
2. I've referenced religion from time to time. I've found, anecdotally, that as people age, they tend to either return to or find religion of one sort or another. I make no value judgments but only suggest that you shouldn't be embarrassed by that quest.
3. "For 75 Years Helping to Keep Planes Aloft," *New York Times*, July 18, 2017.

Epilog

I've found that one of the primary ways to create and sustain healthy change and maintain a productive life is through character. To me, character is about personal strength, moral fiber, and resilience. It's the determination to do the right thing, fight the good fight, and never give up on a worthy cause. It's far better to fail in a noble pursuit than it is to succeed in an ignoble one.

In building the life, career, and contribution you want to be worthy of at threescore and more, you need to build character. That's right, *build* character. In our book *Lifestorming*, my coauthor Marshall Goldsmith and I identified six resource areas that contribute to building character.[1] As our life's journey progresses, we need to continually examine these and deliberately build on them, because as we grow, we improve, and as we improve, the bar rises still more, and as the bar rises, our character must improve to meet higher challenges.

My strong suggestion is that, to instantiate what you've already read in this book, pay close attention to building your character and you'll be in demand and greatly appreciated at any age.

Character Components

The following are the generally acknowledged components in psychological literature of what we call "character." Note that they are specific and can be built, sustained, and applied daily.

1. **Intelligence.** The ability to apply critical thinking skills to problems and challenges. Separating how one thinks about something from what one feels about it. Aptitude for learning. The ability to quickly discern and apply patterns and identify distinctions.

2. **Drive or assertiveness.** The ability to identify the need for and to create urgency. A goal orientation. Moving through and around obstacles that block others. Finding ways to make something happen rather than creating excuses about why something can't happen.

3. **Happiness.** Akin to Dan Gilbert's work at Harvard,[2] this isn't merely about births, victories, birthdays, and weddings, but our ability to create "synthetic" happiness (which we often dismiss negatively as "rationalization"). My getting fired *was* one of the best things that ever happened to me, just as a broken arm, a car crash, or a missed flight may be one of yours. Seeking and achieving well-being on our own terms is an essential aspect of character.

4. **Empathy.** The ability to put yourself in another's shoes and understand how he or she feels. The extension of kindness—goodness—and genuine regard for others is a wonderful character trait. This is why passive-aggressive behavior (remember: "Your daughter was accepted at Michigan? Congratulations. I assume that was her backup school?") reflects weak character, because it is malicious and seeks to subtly undermine others.

5. **Reciprocity and friendship.** The ability to give as well as take, to contribute as much as benefit. Introversion is not a negative, but the unwillingness to help others and to create friendships is. Healthy people maintain friendships; although, as we discussed earlier, some of

these may and should change as one's circumstances do, which is why we're also pointing out that character is never static.

6. **Intimacy and trust.** The ability to form loving bonds and to allow for vulnerability. The people we coach who make the most progress the fastest are those who are comfortable exposing their fears and weaknesses—to be vulnerable in front of others. People incapable of creating strong, intimate bonds in their lives are affected by a key character flaw.

I hope that leaving you with these building blocks will help you transition from my words today to your behaviors tomorrow.

Notes

1. Alan Weiss and Marshall Goldsmith, *Lifestorming,* Wiley, Hoboken, NJ, 2017.
2. Dan Gilbert, *Stumbling on Happiness,* Knopf, New York, 2007.

About the Author

Alan Weiss is one of those rare people who can say he is a consultant, speaker, and author and mean it. His consulting firm, Summit Consulting Group, Inc., has attracted clients such as Merck, Hewlett-Packard, GE, Mercedes-Benz, State Street Corporation, Times Mirror Group, the Federal Reserve, The New York Times Company, Toyota, and more than 500 other leading organizations. He has served on the boards of directors of the Trinity Repertory Company, a Tony Award–winning New England regional theater, Festival Ballet, and the Elizabeth Buffum Chace Center for Battered Women, and has chaired the Newport International Film Festival.

His speaking typically includes 20 keynotes a year at major conferences, and he has been a visiting faculty member at Case Western Reserve University, Boston College, Tufts, St. John's, the University of Illinois, Johnson and Wales University, the Institute of Management Studies, and the University of Georgia Graduate School of Business. He has held an appointment as adjunct professor in the Graduate School of Business at the University of Rhode Island, where he taught courses on advanced management and consulting skills. He once held the record for selling out the highest-priced workshop (on entrepreneurialism) in the then-21-year history of New York City's Learning Annex. His PhD is in psychology. He has served on the Board of Governors of Harvard University's Center for Mental Health and the Media.

He is an inductee into the Professional Speaking Hall of Fame® and the concurrent recipient of the National Speakers Association Council of

Peers Award of Excellence, representing the top 1 percent of professional speakers in the world. He has been named a Fellow of the Institute of Management Consultants, one of only two people in history holding both those designations.

His prolific publishing includes more than 500 articles and 60 books, including his 25-year best seller, *Million Dollar Consulting* (McGraw-Hill). His most recent prior to this book is *Lifestorming* (with Marshall Goldsmith, Wiley). His books have been on the curricula at Villanova, Temple University, and the Wharton School of Business, and have been translated into 13 languages.

He is interviewed and quoted frequently in the media. His career has taken him to 60 countries and 49 states. (He is afraid to go to North Dakota.) *Success Magazine* cited him in an editorial devoted to his work as "a worldwide expert in executive education." The *New York Post* called him "one of the most highly regarded independent consultants in America." He is the winner of the prestigious AXIEM Award for Excellence in Audio Presentation.

He is the recipient of the Lifetime Achievement Award of the American Press Institute, the first ever for a nonjournalist, and one of only seven awarded in the 65-year history of the association. He holds an annual Thought Leadership Conference, which draws global experts as his guests. In 2017, his featured speaker was Harvard distinguished professor Dan Gilbert, whose work on happiness has drawn over 15 million TED views.

He has coached Miss Rhode Island/Miss America candidates in interviewing skills. He once appeared on the popular American TV game show *Jeopardy*, where he lost badly in the first round to a dancing waiter from Iowa.

Alan has been married to the lovely Maria for 49 years, and they have two children and twin granddaughters. They reside in East Greenwich, Rhode Island, with their dogs, Coco (a Cavapoo) and Bentley (a white German Shepherd).

Index